Composers of Wales
2

Editor: Roy Bol

Basil Deane

Alun Hoddinott

University of Wales Press
on behalf of the Welsh Arts Council

1978

Printed in Wales
by D. Brown and Sons, Ltd.

CONTENTS

PREFACE

In presenting a study of the music of a living composer who is still in mid-career I have conceived my task to be primarily one of introduction rather than critical assessment. Accordingly I have touched on as wide a range of the music as space permits, and have avoided extensive analysis, while suggesting lines of analytical approach which may be pursued and developed by the interested specialist.

I should like to record my gratitude to the Music Department of Oxford University Press. Not only did they make their scores available to me; they were always ready to reorganise themselves to afford me space to work on their premises in Conduit Street. I am also grateful to the Executors of James Joyce's Estate and the publishers Jonathan Cape Limited for permission to reproduce the paragraph from James Joyce, *A Portrait of the Artist as a Young Man*, on page 32. I am deeply indebted to Alun Hoddinott who, with characteristic generosity, gave me free access to all his unpublished material. In the belief that, in general, composers should be left to compose, I did not consult him about the contents of this book. For the facts, opinions and analyses it contains I must therefore take sole responsibility.

I INTRODUCTION

Alun Hoddinott was born at Bargoed, Glamorgan, on 11 August 1929. He attended Gowerton Grammar School, and in 1946 won a music scholarship to University College, Cardiff. He entered the music department, and during his undergraduate years he also studied privately with the composer Arthur Benjamin in London. He graduated BMus in 1949. In 1951 he was appointed to the Cardiff (now Welsh) College of Music and Drama, and in the same year won the Arnold Bax medal for composition. In 1959 he returned to University College as a lecturer, and the degree of DMus was conferred upon him in the following year. He was made Reader in Music in 1963, and four years later he succeeded Joseph Morgan as Professor of Music at Cardiff, a post he still holds. His influence upon Welsh musical life has extended well beyond the University, and as artistic director of the Cardiff Festival of 20th century music he has played a major rôle in the promotion of contemporary music in South Wales.

These are the main biographical facts. An apparently straightforward case, it would seem, of a composer with strong roots in his native soil, studying, maturing and working in a familiar environment. Overt nationalism in music is out of fashion, and we should hardly expect a succession of works directly inspired, in the 19th century manner, by the landscape and legends of the principality. But Hoddinott's consistent allegiance to his native environment is not fortuitous. He is, by choice as well as by birth, a Welsh composer.

The statement is easier to make than to define. Hoddinott has drawn predominantly on Welsh authors for the texts of his vocal compositions. But few of his instrumental works have Welsh connotations. The exceptions, such as the sets of *Welsh Dances* for orchestra, are occasional pieces and, in their style, untypical of the composer. His usual idiom, unlike those of Bartók and Vaughan Williams, owes nothing to folk elements. Nor is there any tradition of Welsh art music to which his work can be related. Hoddinott's Welshness is intrinsic, not external. The national flavour of his music derives from his own personality; it is a matter of mood rather than material, of atmosphere rather than structure. There are dominant characteristics in Hoddinott's music which betray a Celtic rather than an Anglo-Saxon temperament: obsessive drive, sombre brooding, rhetorical lyricism, fiery outbursts, and, embracing all these, a love of language itself, a delight in virtuosic manipulation of the means of communication.

There is another aspect of the composer's personality which is also of great importance in his work. Like other Northern artists before him, Hoddinott, who is an enthusiastic traveller, is attracted to Southern Europe, and to Italy in particular. It is there that he has spent many working vacations, and some of his major compositions have been conceived and planned in Italy. Every musician is of course aware of the Italian heritage, and most composers are indebted, directly or indirectly, to Italy, for the forms and techniques developed there. But Hoddinott's commitment is a deeper, more personal one. The clear

9

skies of the Mediterranean are as essential to him as is the temperate climate of Britain. These contrasting attractions are not mutually exclusive. On the contrary, they induce a tension which seeks resolution through creation. The dualism symbolized by these two geographical influences is at the heart of Hoddinott's work. His music is, as a rule, complex. But the complexity is never arbitrary; it is born of an ability, indeed a compulsion, to see things from different angles, to explore the interactions of separate forces, to reshape material in the light of other events.

One of the most obvious manifestations of Hoddinott's sympathy with the Italian tradition is his preference for formal shapes deriving from the procedures of the Italian Baroque rather than the sonata forms of the 19th century Austro-German symphonic succession. And in another fundamental respect he is closer to the Baroque than to the Romantic age. Like the Baroque musician he regards composition as a craft, and is capable of writing as and when circumstances dictate, within imposed limits of time and specification. Much of his work is commissioned, and his output—over one hundred compositions, most of substantial dimensions—is impressive by contemporary standards. He has contributed to every major category of composition: orchestral and chamber music; vocal music, ranging from solo songs to large scale choral works; music for the theatre, including full-length opera. Such fluency and versatility carry the concomitant risks of superficiality and repetitiousness. But Hoddinott has minimized these dangers by developing an idiom which is at once personal and at the same time flexible enough to allow for adaptation to each set of compositional circumstances. His language is consistent as well as distinctive—there is a 'Hoddinott sound' which is identifiable in all periods of his writing. But there has also been a steady evolution of style as his expressive needs have developed. He has never been content to repeat himself. Inevitably, some works, related by date or medium, have recognizable points of resemblance, or even, in his recent composition, intentional cross-reference. But in its detail each work has its own pattern, its own feeling, and each makes its own contribution to the totality of the *oeuvre*.

From the beginning of his composing career Hoddinott displayed a sure-footed self-confidence amid the criss-cross paths of 20th century musical styles. He has withdrawn his student compositions, including a cello concerto, a symphonic suite, and two string quartets. But the first work in his orchestral catalogue, the Concerto for clarinet and string orchestra of 1950, shows no sign of hesitancy or immaturity. The idiom is of a type fairly widespread at the time. The three movements, Capriccio, Arioso, Burletta, are formally straight-forward, light-textured, and basically tonal in harmony. The potential of the composer is indicated by the imaginative handling of the instrumental resources, limited as they are, and by the quality of the melodic invention.

The orchestral *Nocturne* of 1952 marks another stage in Hoddinott's development. The choice of title is itself significant. The concept of the Nocturne evolved from the piano pieces of Chopin, expressions of mood rather than painting, through the sensuous evocations of Debussy to the mysterious world of nocturnal sound and stillness conjured up by Bartók's 'night-music' movements. Hoddinott owes something to each of these composers while remaining distinctively individual. Like Chopin, he creates a dominant melodic line, one that develops on the principle of internal motivic variation, so that different phases of the line are interrelated (Ex 1a). He shares Debussy's interest in textural subtlety, and the merging of orchestral colours. And he adopts one of Bartók's favourite shapes, the modified ternary or 'arch' form. The movement opens with quiet notes on the horns emerging from a *pp* string chord, reaches a powerful climax and then continues with a free restatement of the material, including inversion of some of the melodic phrases (Ex 1b), before dissolving into the silence of the beginning.

Ex. 1

The principle of the arch as a structural element came to play an increasingly important part in Hoddinott's compositional thinking, and from the use of inversion he moved logically to the palindrome, a statement in which the second half is a reversal of the first (a well-known verbal example is 'Able was I ere I saw Elba'). The parallel between architecture and music has often (perhaps too often) been drawn, and, if architecture is frozen music, music is structure in time. But events in the dimensions of space and time impose quite different modes of perception. An arch is perceived simultaneously as an entity, and its principal effect is one of symmetry. Music is apprehended successively, and the notion of symmetry is at best an analogy. Ternary and sonata forms, despite their ABA shape, are not inherently symmetrical in the architectural sense. A composition in one of these forms ends, not at its starting point, but at the end of the restatement of the first main section. The closest analogy to architectural symmetry is one in which the music both returns to and ends with its point of departure, and this implies a reversed or palindromic restatement in the second half of the piece or movement.

Such a technique of reversed restatement is only possible in certain circumstances. An idiom heavily dependant on the vertical or harmonic aspect does not lend itself easily to reversal, since thereby the chordal sequence is radically altered. For that reason there are very few examples written between 1600 and 1900, and those that do exist are essentially *jeux d'esprit* on the part of the composers. On the other hand a style which is primarily horizontal or melodic, whose vertical aspect is secondary or incidental, may very well allow for palindromic treatment. Such was the case in the 14th century, and the French composer Guillaume de Machaut was able to illustrate the medieval paradox 'My end is my beginning, and my beginning my end' in a musical setting which is a double palindrome. Hoddinott's idiom, too, became increasingly melody-centred and independent of chordal movement, so he was able to adopt the palindrome as a major technical element. Early

Ex. 2

Ex. 3

examples are to be found in the third movement (Notturno) of the Oboe Concerto (1955) and the first movement of the Septet (1956) (Exx 2 and 3). In these cases it is only the main theme which is restated in palindrome. In later works, such as the Concerto for piano, wind and percussion (1960), Hoddinott extended the palindrome over an entire movement. The advantages and the limitations of a completely symmetrical structure are apparent in the first movement of this concerto. The music moves towards a massive climax at the central point of the movement, and thereafter the reversed statement progressively reduces the tension, over the same span of time. But it is psychologically desirable that the climax should occur nearer the end than the beginning of the movement, and that the process of relaxation should be quicker than that of the preceding build-up of tension. So Hoddinott frequently modifies his palindromic structures in various ways. In the first movement of the Second Symphony the overall shape is the same as that of the Concerto. But the climax, which involves a reiteration of the opening motif, is followed by a condensed palindromic version of its melodic outline, and in this way a more rapid descent from the climax is achieved. Moreover the end, although palindromically exact as to pitch, is a *pp* version of the *ff* opening. Other treatments include the insertion of a non-palindromic central section, with the climax delayed (e.g. the first movement of the Harp Concerto), and compression of the restatement. The palindrome has continued to be a major component of Hoddinott's technique; most of his principal works written before 1970 contain at least one example. In his most recent compositions, however, there are signs that he is relying less frequently on this device.

The fifties saw another development in Hoddinott's work: a move towards the use of a note set. His idiom remained tonally based; but chordal patterns were replaced by free movement around one or more tonal centres, represented by a note rather than a chordal grouping. The melodic lines became more chromatic, and some of the resultant phrases took on a twelve-note character. This development led Hoddinott to the more formal application of note sets in the early sixties, and since then they have been a central element in his technique. His use of the set is not in any sense Schoenbergian. It is not intended to inhibit a sense of tonal movement, and it does not govern the harmonic dimension. It is rather a primary source of varied melodic material. Hoddinott's themes, as John McCabe has pointed out, 'derive from a kind of perpetual variation of small motifs, characterized principally by certain intervals which are perhaps the organic centre of the material'.[1] So he treats the set as a nucleus of short interlocking motifs, each with its characteristic interval formation, and each capable of development in its own right, independent of its original context. These points may be illustrated by examples drawn from *Sinfonietta 2* (Ex 4). The set itself is internally structured, the second half being a transposed inversion of the first (Ex 4a). Conspicuous is the 3-note motif *x*, juxtaposing the intervals of the perfect and the augmented fourth. The extracts that follow exemplify the inventive flexibility with which the composer handles the set (transpositions of the set are assumed). Ex 4b is the opening of the work, and presents the set simultaneously in original and in inverted form. Later in the first movement Hoddinott achieves a chromatic ascending

Ex. 4

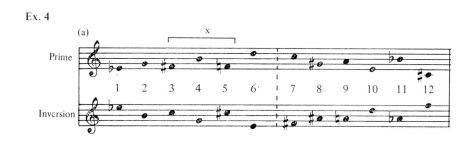

[1] Record sleeve note on recording of String Quartet and Clarinet Sonata (GSGC 14107).

Ex. 4

motif by treating two notes as acciaccatura (4c). The quick second movement opens with a theme built from *x* (4d), while later the first four notes form a sequentially rising pattern (4e). In the third movement the melodic line again derives largely from *x*, but here assumes a static hypnotic character, with the intervals F sharp-B, B-F natural providing 'the organic centre of the material' and the tonal centre as well (4f). The short fourth movement is based on a free improvisation on the notes of the set. The concluding Presto theme uses various motifs from the set, with special attention to the fourths of *x* (4g), a feature that receives additional emphasis in the palindromic restatement. As the conclusion approaches, a new bass theme emerges, derived from the set, but altered to underline E flat, the tonic note of the whole work (4h).

The melodic patterns evolve against a harmonic background. This is generated independently of the basic set, although the nature of the two structures is such that there may be a degree of coincident relationship between them. In the earlier works the dissonance content results from chromatic alteration or addition applied to an essentially triadic chord (Ex 5). Later harmonic combinations are more complex, and generally involve superposition of intervallic groups of two or three notes on different pitch levels. In Sinfonietta 2 the initial melodic statement of the set (Ex 4b) is accompanied by this chord, which is built from the superposition of a major second combination (or, alternatively, it could be regarded as two diminished sevenths a major second apart) (Ex 6). In the second movement an extended passage is spread over this progression, each chord of which combines two dominant sevenths (Ex 7). The Fourth Symphony also begins with a chord constructed

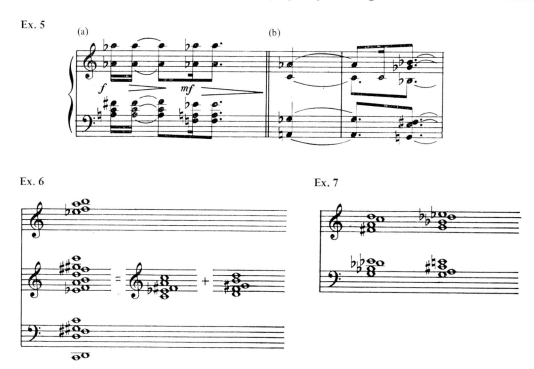

Ex. 5   (a)   (b)

Ex. 6   Ex. 7

on the transposition of the three-note group, containing a minor third and a perfect fourth (F sharp, A, B). In the second chord the perfect fourth becomes a diminished fourth (F sharp, A, B flat), and the pitch levels of the groups are altered, resulting in a chord containing all twelve semitones (Ex 8). A similarly constructed chord in *The sun, the great luminary of the universe* finds resolution in a major triad (Ex 9). Sometimes there is a differentiation between the structural basis of neighbouring discords, which has, exceptionally, a thematic function. The opening three chords of *Variants*, which subsequently generate melodic material, are built on thirds, fourths, and the tritone respectively (Ex 10).

The danger implicit in such elaborate chord structures is that their individual character will remain undifferentiated and their sequence sound purely arbitrary. Hoddinott guards against these risks by carefully planning both the lay-out within each chord in relation to the participating instruments, and the movement from one chord to another, so that changes of content and therefore of character and function become perceptible. The chords thereby contribute to the function of establishing or suspending a sense of tonal security. Like Bartók, for instance, Hoddinott generally bases his large-scale harmonic structures on the tension between tonal centres, and, again as in the case of his predecessor, these are often a tritone apart. The chords are assisted in their defining function by other means. Inevitably pedal devices play an essential rôle. These include single notes, sustained or repeated in a striking rhythmic pattern; ostinato figures, often rhythmically irregular; repeated chordal groups with a strong focal character; and any combination of these techniques.

Hoddinott's rhythmic procedures are related to other structural aspects of the music. Rhythmic shapes variously delay, suspend, qualify or emphasise the underlying metrical pattern. At the start of a composition the definition of the prevailing metre may be postponed by avoidance of regular grouping or equal note-values. Here is an abstraction of the rhythmic framework from the beginning of the Fourth Symphony (Ex 11). Melodies, especially in slower sections, often contain complex sub-divisions of the note values, and ties and syncopations, which efface the sense of metre, as in this unaccompanied phrase for flute from *Fioriture* (Ex 12). Even in more strongly metrical contexts the same devices

Ex. 11

Ex. 12

overlay the metre, creating a rhythmic counterpoint; this is particularly common in the trio sections of scherzo movements, as in this example from the Third Symphony (Ex 13). At other times the rhythm is apparently straightforward. A feature of the composer's style is a triple time scherzo melody, whose even crotchet rhythm contrasts with its angular melodic outline (Ex 14). Irregular metres may also characterize the statement of a theme, but these are rarely maintained over longer stretches (v. Ex 22). Many of Hoddinott's themes have in fact a strong rhythmic configuration, which does play a distinctive part in the extended development of a section or a movement.

The overall relationships of sections and movements is another matter to which Hoddinott attaches considerable significance. In his earlier works he adopted the looser formal associations of the Baroque in preference to the four-movement symphonic layout.

Ex. 13

Ex. 14

When he did use four movements, they were often in a slow-quick-slow-quick sequence (First Piano Sonata, Violin Concerto). More usually the ternary shape of individual movements was reflected in the overall structure, either in a quick-slow-quick sequence (Clarinet Concerto, Septet), or its inversion, slow-quick-slow (First Symphony, Concerto for piano, wind and percussion, Viola Concertino). Other works showed an adaptation of the suite principle, with a larger number of shorter movements, some of them in several sections (Sextet, Divertimento). In his later works Hoddinott has continued this formal exploration, and in consequence the compositions display on the one hand an unusually wide range of formal profiles, and at the same time a recurrence and development of certain structural tendencies in works separated by date of composition or by medium. One structural area which has undergone considerable evolution is that of variation. It is of course true that the application of the same note set to more than one movement of the same work implies a variation technique. But the variation principle is important to Hoddinott in a more specific sense. Two fairly early sets illustrate two different modes of approach. In the Variations for flute, clarinet, harp and string quartet (1962), despite the common source of material, the individual sections are very strongly characterized as small scale examples of larger forms, e.g. March, Nocturne, Scherzo, etc. In the Divertimento of the following year an eight bar theme and its variations form a continuous movement, with a concluding return of the theme. The first type is carried much further in the orchestral *Variants* of 1966, whose six contrasted movements (which include a set of variations) are interrelated in a more complex way, so that the effect is, in the composer's words, 'of a double set of variants running out of parallel'. The second type is developed in such different contexts as the second movement of the Organ Concerto and the Episodi which concludes the Second Violin Sonata. A variation technique is often implicitly at work in other contexts, as in the First Violin Sonata, consisting of eleven short sections, all derived from common material which is never explicitly stated, but is present 'as a shadowy background' (AH). Variation techniques enable the composer to extend his exploration of the potentialities of his basic material over the widest canvas, and recently Hoddinott has found it necessary to move beyond the frame of a single work. The four chamber compositions of Op. 78, for example, derive their material from the same note set; while his work on the recent song cycle *Landscapes* gave birth to three orchestral pieces with the same title.

Like other composers in the sixties Hoddinott was concerned to reconcile the individual performer's capacity for spontaneous improvisation with predetermined shapes, lines and textures. Not surprisingly it was the concerto form which provided the initial stimulus, and the movements of the Harp Concerto of 1957 are entitled Dialogue, Improvisation and Fantasy. Although the score is fully determined, the overall impression is one of a strongly improvisatory character. (The harp is evidently a favourite instrument of Hoddinott's, and the same approach to it marks the later pieces for solo harp, including the Sonata, the Suite and the Fantasy). The *locus classicus* of improvisatory self-expression is the cadenza, and it is accorded the status of a separate movement in several works. The Third Piano Concerto, the Clarinet Sonata and the Second Violin Sonata begin with movements entitled Cadenza, and the Horn Concerto ends with one. The First Violin Sonata includes a section marked Allegro quasi cadenza, and the first movement of the Cello Sonata ends with an extended example. The freedom of the cadenza is associated with a more formal structure in the Nocturne and Cadenzas for clarinet, violin and cello, and Hoddinott explores this relationship further in the Nocturnes and Cadenzas for cello and orchestra. Occasionally improvisatory elements form a part of an otherwise predetermined texture. In the Second Violin Sonata, for example, a thematic statement is accompanied by a rhythmically free ostinato, consisting of part of the note set and its inversion (Ex 15). Similar liberty of

Ex. 15

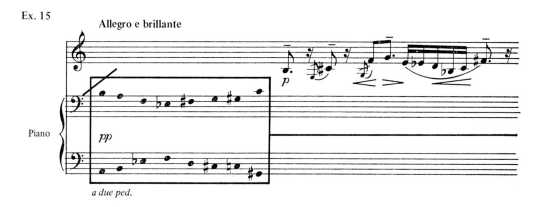

rhythmic interpretation occurs also in the later orchestral works (e.g. *Fioriture*, Symphony no. 3, Sinfonietta 2). But the function of such passages is generally to establish a background wash of sound, and aleatoric procedures have remained a subordinate, albeit significant, element in Hoddinott's music.

Instrumental colour and texture have come to occupy an increasingly important part in the composer's thinking, especially in the orchestral works. Hoddinott has always composed directly on to a full score. His music is not 'orchestrated'; the ideas are associated from their inception with particular instruments or sections of the orchestra. From his earliest works he evinces a confident command of orchestral colour, and shows distinct preferences for certain instrumental registers, combinations and textures; for example, flutes and clarinets in their lowest register, bassoons in the upper compass; closely woven brass 'choirs' in the tenor region, accompanying high unison or octave-doubled strings. But perhaps the most striking aspect of his instrumentation has been his developing interest in the potential of the percussion section. This predilection was already evident in the First Piano Concerto, whose accompaniment includes such high tuned percussion as vibraphone, xylophone, glockenspiel and celesta, as well as an extensive array of untuned percussion. *Variants* was also, in this respect as in others, a landmark. The score calls for five percussion players in addition to timpani, celesta and harp, and the large battery of percussion impresses its own extensive range of colour upon the whole work. This expanded rôle of the percussion is also a major factor in subsequent works such as the Organ Concerto, *Fioriture* and the Fourth Symphony. In the *scena* for solo soprano and instrumental ensemble, *Roman Dream* (1968), the percussion writing reaches a peak of elaboration and virtuosity. Allied to this development is the exploration of instrumental texture *per se* as the main compositional element in an orchestral work. Hoddinott's music is never athematic or completely atonal. But in such scores as *Night Music* (1966) and *The sun, the great luminary of the universe* (1970) the actual note pitches appear to be almost incidental to the evolution and interplay of the various textures.

II THE SYMPHONIES AND OTHER ORCHESTRAL WORKS

Although the symphony no longer holds the central position that it occupied in late 19th and early 20th century music, it still offers a special challenge to the composer interested in large-scale orchestral composition. Hoddinott has not allocated to the symphony a uniquely pre-eminent place in his work; but he has returned to the form at different stages of his career. The Symphony no. 1 dates from 1955, and is the first large-scale orchestral work in his catalogue. In both scale and content it marks a new departure in his work. It is scored for full orchestra, with triple wind, and lasts thirty-five minutes in performance. The three movements are: Adagio, Allegro assai, Grave. In each Hoddinott demonstrates his ability to apply his characteristic techniques on a larger canvas. The first movement reflects the overall arch shape of the whole work; its curve rises from pp in a controlled crescendo to the central climax, then subsides to a quietly inconclusive end. In the middle movement the principal theme, a quick, twisting melody on the violas, gives birth to numerous variants, whose individuality is as unmistakeable as is their common parentage (Ex 16). The weighty climax at the end of the Grave illustrates the composer's assured handling of his copious orchestral forces. Although the work as a whole does not present the closely woven textures and the taut structures of some of its successors, it is nonetheless a valuable achievement, and a pointer to subsequent development.

The Symphony no. 2 is one of several works dedicated to Alan Rawsthorne. Rawsthorne encouraged and helped the younger musician, and the two men were close personal friends until Rawthorne's death. This personal relationship was founded upon mutual affinities

Ex. 16

21

and understanding, and it might be assumed that it would lead to specific cross-influences in compositional style. It is indeed apparent that Rawsthorne and Hoddinott have points of contact in their work. They both prefer the more weighty forms, although both are also capable of exploiting a lighter vein, as the *Street Corner Overture* and the *Welsh Dances* testify. And there are some technical features which suggest a common outlook: their liking for the dark, hollow sounds of the lower woodwind; or the characteristic Rawsthorne motifs which combine the intervals of a minor second and a minor third, outlines often matched by the germinal motifs in Hoddinott's note sets. But the differences are equally important. Hoddinott's language is the more fluent, more flexible (although not on that account necessarily more expressive), and his capacity for absorption of new stylistic elements is more evident, so that his idiom shows a greater degree of evolution than that of Rawsthorne. It may well be that contact with Rawsthorne and his music enabled Hoddinott to realize his own musical personality more fully, and it is in this sense rather than in specific technical matters that Rawsthorne acted as an influence upon him, while leaving him entirely free to express his own individuality.

Nowhere does Hoddinott declare this individuality more strikingly than in the opening bars of a work. The first movement of the Second Symphony is an Adagio, and it is launched by a *ff* unison quintuplet figure acting as an anacrusis to the sustained D of the second bar (Ex 17). This memorable gesture not only establishes D as the keynote; it also

Ex. 17

implants in the listener's consciousness the opening C sharp. The tonic D dies away, and a searching chromatic line emerges in the lower strings, punctuated by irregularly spaced chordal groups. This line evolves without direct repetition or sequence; but certain intervallic shapes become prominent. The texture is austere, the orchestration sombre. A crescendo builds to a massive, extended restatement of the initial anacrusis and resolution. The rest of the movement is a palindromic restatement of the first part, ending on a quiet suspensive C sharp.

In several respects this movement characterizes the composer's approach to structural matters. The arch form is a common one, and was indeed a feature of the First Symphony. But the treatment of it here is far from stereotyped. The tonic D, so strongly affirmed at the outset, is the starting-point for a harmonic exploration. But in this instance the emerging melodic line does not arrive at another fixed tonal point. The central return to D gives the impression not of resolution, but of reiteration or restatement of a base whose influence has never been superseded. It is in the second part of the movement that this influence wanes, and the final C sharp leaves the issue uncertain. So the fundamental nature of the movement is opposed to that of a sonata-form structure, whose evolution and subsequent resolution are the consequence of movement away from the influence of the home tonic to another key centre. It appears to symbolize not conflict but rather a painful struggle to escape from the control of a powerful and inhibiting force, an impression heightened when the opening motif reasserts itself at a climax in the following movement.

The same sense of movement around a fixed point is reinforced by the beginning of the second movement, Allegro molto. The focus here is on G, and the opening phrases cling to it, with close, mainly semitonal movement (Ex 18). Later material has the same intensive,

Ex. 18

reiterative quality, deriving from internal motivic repetition, stepwise movement, and tied note syncopations. The overall structure combines palindromic and rondo elements. One episode displays contrapuntal textures typical of the composer: rhythmically close but melodic free imitations between the several strands. The Molto Adagio also recalls the first movement, in that an essentially melodic texture develops into a heavily reiterated chordal climax in which the notes of the chromatic scale accumulate, until all twelve are sounding at once. This tremendous outburst is followed by a quiet coda of Webernesque simplicity and austerity, referring back to the opening, and the final chord leaves the harmonic basis of the movement unresolved (Ex 19).

Ex. 19

The last movement, Maestoso-Allegro-Maestoso-Presto, is a scherzo with trio, framed by an introduction and a coda. The main theme, stated on woodwind, recalls Hindemith in its march-like character, its melodic and rhythmic contours, and its instrumental colour. It is expanded and developed, with easily recognisable variants and inversions of the material. The trio begins quietly with unaccompanied melodic curves interspersed by distant fanfares in the wind; these fanfares borrow their triplet rhythm from the opening section, their harmonic ambiguity from the slow movement. They become more and more prominent as the climax point leading to the return of the first section is reached.

Just as the melodic material is more forthright and sharply defined than that of the earlier movements, so too the tonal situation clarifies. The A flat heard at the beginning of the principal theme (Ex 20) now becomes an opposing tonal centre to the home D. The

Ex. 20

recapitulation begins with the theme transposed an augmented fourth higher, and just before the coda another climax is reached, presenting simultaneously the chords of D major and A flat major. It is only in the concluding bars of the work that this tension is definitively resolved in an affirmation of D major.

The Third Symphony postdates the Second by six years. The most immediately perceptible point of stylistic difference for the listener is the range of the orchestral palette. By 1968 Hoddinott's interest in extending the scope of the percussion section had become manifest, and this score calls for a wide assortment of percussion instruments, ranging from claves, bongos and maracas, to chime bars, bells and vibraphone, and including a piano. The resulting timbres are inventively applied in a great variety of combinations with the more usual instrumental colours, adding a new dimension to the orchestral sonorities. Related to this increased emphasis on colour as an important design factor is the introduction of a semi-aleatoric section, in which note groups are repeated in free rhythms as an accompaniment to a thematic statement at an important moment of climax in the first movement.

In other respects the continuity of Hoddinott's thought is manifest. The disposition of the two movements, Adagio-Presto and Allegro-Adagio, makes an arch form, and the material of the concluding section is a reworking and a resolution of the first Adagio. The opening motto theme, consisting of low-pitched B flat reiterated in irregular rhythm, is again of crucial importance for the whole work (Ex 21). As in the last movement of No. 2,

Ex. 21

Hoddinott uses the tritone as the basis of tonal conflict; in this instance the B flat-E relationship is postulated from the beginning, with four statements of the motto theme, two on B flat and two on E, providing the framework of the Adagio. A march-like theme emerging from the motto, which is at first ominous, and later threatening, underlines the tonal tension. Before the end of the section a new theme focussed on B flat is adumbrated in the bass under oscillating wind chords. This composite idea becomes an important element of the following Presto, which is again a scherzo with trio. The first theme is also fixed on B flat; it is irregular in metre and top and bottom form a mirror image by inversion (Ex 22). The rhythm of the motto theme and its two original pitches provide the basis for the trio section. The return of the scherzo is modified and shortened, and its dissonant harmony remains unresolved.

Ex. 22

The second movement begins on E. Jagged broken figures clash with one another in tense counterpoint, encouraged by violent interjections from the percussion. But the main climax is attained by the expansion of a texture, rhythmically fluid, which begins quietly in the broad melodic phrases drawn against a background of scurrying string figures. It is fairly rare in Hoddinott to find long passages based on unchanging ostinato figures; this crescendo by accumulation is one of the most striking. The returning Adagio is altered to reassert the tonic without equivocation, and in the tranquil closing bars the dissonant E is absorbed into a B flat chord.

The Fourth Symphony followed closely on the Third, and, like the latter, was first performed by the Hallé Orchestra, in 1969. Once again Hoddinott chooses to begin with a slow movement, and a comparison with the corresponding Adagio of the Second Symphony shows the direction in which the composer's thinking has evolved. In the earlier work the dominant melodic lines is distinctively drawn, the rhythmic impulse is clearly defined, the textures are sparser, the colours unambiguous. In the Fourth Symphony Adagio these elements are handled in a much more complex manner. The opening is a matrix from which the various constituents gradually emerge and take shape. Long sustained chords, built on F sharp and held by wind and strings divided into as many as twenty-six parts, establish a rich web of sound which characterizes the entire movement. Irregular patterns on timpani and the avoidance of accented beats for melodic and harmonic movement create a sense of rhythmic indeterminacy. The melodic outlines are obscured by simultaneous use of moving and sustaining parts in the same compass and within the same orchestral group (Ex 23). The tuned percussion lend individual colour to the separate notes and harmonies. As the movement evolves ideas momentarily take more definite shape and direction, but the overall impression is one of creative flux. In its scale, scope and kaleidoscopic detail this is one of Hoddinott's most fascinating slow movements.

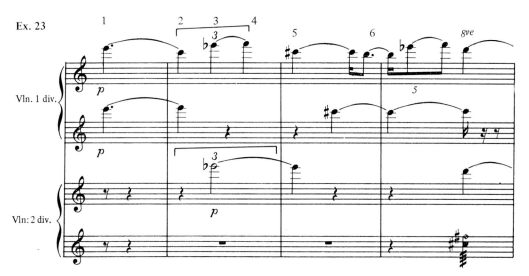

The Presto is in extreme contrast. Tonality, rhythm and melody are aggressively asserted. The F sharp of the opening is now reiterated in a short rhythmic figure by the strings, alternating with a woodwind phrase which expands with each repetition (Ex 24). This paragraph is succeeded by another in which the strings reaffirm their commitment to F sharp, while the wind reply with their original figure inverted. In the altered restatement the music moves from the keynote F sharp, although the rhythmic figure associated with it continues to dominate the texture. The following Allegro, whose opening theme is another variant of the basic set (c.f. Exx 23, 24, 25), does nothing to restore the tonal centre. In general character it is not unlike the corresponding movement of the Third Symphony. It is only with the concluding Maestoso that the tonic is re-established, and the whole symphony resolved into the quiet profundity of the opening sounds.

The Fifth Symphony dates from 1973, and is in two movements, and testifies to the composer's continuing interest in formal experimentation. The opening Allegro combines passacaglia and ritornello elements. The varied appearances of the passacaglia material, usually lightly scored, are introduced and linked by the ritornello idea on the full orchestration, itself also varied.

The second movement is another adaptation of variation form, on similar, although not identical, lines to the earlier *Variants*. It consists of six sections described by the composer as 'reflective panels':

| 1 Adagio | 3 Andante | 5 Adagio |
| 2 Allegretto | 4 Allegro | 6 Presto |

The panels are complementary, 1 + 6, 2 + 5 and 3 + 4 being related thematically. Material from the first movement is also integrated into this movement, in accordance with Hoddinott's increasingly frequent practice of treating the finale as a summing up of the whole work.

The five symphones are full-length works, calling for large orchestral forces. Mindful of the place in orchestral programming for smaller scale compositions Hoddinott has also established what he himself has described as a 'continuing series of short abstract orchestral works', the Sinfoniettas. He has written four Sinfoniettas since 1968. They share some general family resemblance; they are all about ten to twelve minutes long, and they are scored for an orchestra of basically double woodwind dimensions. And the composer's comment on no. 2 is, to some extent, applicable to them all: 'the aim of the work is to divert'. Each nevertheless retains an individual physiognomy, expressed by modifications to the basic orchestral forces, by distinctive formal structures, and by different expressive characters. No. 1 is the most restrained in colour. The opening Rapsodia is predominantly lyrical and has only one climax. The second part, entitled Scherzi, consists of four short movements, played without a break, and again the prevailing dynamic level is contained until the final climax. No. 2 is more varied in style, without excessive weight. Developing the conception applied in the second part of no. 1, the composer has written five short movements, again played without interruption, and thematically interlocked. He has added extra brass, and the percussion section is joined by the harp. The selective use of brass and percussion is important in the texture, and in the penultimate Adagio section the trumpet and percussion are in the foreground of a rhythmically free and changing wash of sound. No. 3 is the most intense and darkly coloured of the series. In the opening Moderato long held chords on lower strings and wind inhibit the lyrical impulse of the violins' melodic line, and lead to a subsequent concentration on the more sombre regions of the orchestra. The same tendency to confine melodic statements to lower brass and woodwind also characterizes the Adagio. A more obviously lively opening to the concluding Allegro leads to a massive central climax which again distinguishes this work from its predecessors. Sinfonietta 4 was written for the National Youth Orchestra of Wales. It is in a lighter vein, with clearly shaped material, and an overall arch form, with a central slow movement in palindrome and a concluding return to the opening material.

Hoddinott has also composed several orchestral works of importance which fall outside these two categories.

Variants, written in 1966, marked a new stage in his development. It is not without significance that the composer, as he himself has pointed out, was stimulated by a summer spent in southern Italy. Moreover he goes on to say, in the introductory note to the score: 'The work is in no sense programmatic but abstract aspects of the Italian scene and its vivid contrasts have helped to fashion the material'.

The work is scored for full orchestra, and is in six movements: 1. Sonata, 2. Toccata, 3. Variazioni, 4. Notturno, 5. Passacaglia, 6. Fuga. Their inter-connection has been described by the composer. 'Movements 1, 3 and 5 present different facets of the same material (i.e. the three chords heard right at the beginning, the first built on thirds, the second on fourths, the third featuring the tritone. The intervals of these chords form a melodic pattern) (v. Ex 10). Movements 2, 4 and 6 each throws back to the immediately preceding movement and are not directly related to each other. Thus the effect is of a double set of variants running out of parallel'. The intricacy of the relationships is heightened by the fact that movement 5 as well as movement 3 is a set of variations. Indeed *Variants* is probably Hoddinott's most structurally complex work; and the freedom and variety with which he handles his material preclude analytical generalizations. Nevertheless a consideration of the individual movements affords an overall view of the composer's techniques at the time of writing.

Sonata is based on two groups of contrasting themes which are 'stated, developed and restated: the first group is fully scored, dramatic and forceful, and the second quietly capricious' (AH.). The restatement is in palindromic form, so the groups are reversed, and the movement ends with a *fff* statement of the generating chords of the opening. The central 'development' contains a new chorale-like passage on trombones and tuba (Ex 26). Violent rhythms, jagged broken figures, and high instrumental tessitura intensify the first group, while the second group phrases are treated in a pointillistic manner, with individual percussion sonorities colouring the texture.

Ex. 26

Toccata, marked Presto, ma sempre sotto voce e leggiero, begins imitatively on the strings, using a theme derived from the opening bars of the first movement (Ex 27). A feeling of tension is given to the swiftly moving texture by small rhythmic irregularities and incidental colouring of the main lines by instrumental doublings. In the central section a wide-spanning melody is drawn against quietly oscillating figuration (Ex 28). The final restatement is both palindromic and transposed.

Ex. 27

Ex. 28

Variazioni consists of twelve short variations, each four bars long, on the three opening chords. They form a continuous movement, reaching a dramatic climax, and falling to a quiet palindromic restatement, with new counterpoint added, of the opening theme. This leads directly into the Notturno, 'a largely static pivot, on which the whole work turns. It is a revolving sequence of sustained chords (the same chords as in the preceding movement) with melodic fragments occasionally illuminated'. The quiet slowly changing chords on wind and divided strings span the entire range of the orchestra's compass, and create a deep, colourless backcloth against which the single notes of the tuned percussion stand out like points of light.

The Passacaglia takes as its theme the brass passage from the first movement (v. Ex 26). In its continuous variation techniques it relates to the previous Variazioni, and it also leads directly into the next movement, Fuga, 'an unstrict double fugue which has also characteristics of the rondo'. Oboe and bassoon share the opening theme, which is derived from the first chord of the Passacaglia (Ex 29). After much playful, and largely uncontrapuntal, treatment of this unfugue-like theme, the Passacaglia theme returns and itself leads to the three opening chords of the work.

Ex. 29

The significance of *Variants* in Hoddinott's evolution lies in this achievement of relating and interlocking forms, patterns and techniques of disparate types to create a large-scale work for orchestra outside the traditional symphonic framework, thus opening up new avenues for future advance. Not only is *Variants* a key work; in its invention and variety it is one of the composer's best scores.

Immediately after *Variants* came *Night Music*, a further exploration of stillness and colour. It is scored for orchestra with double wind and a very large percussion section. The sonorities of the Notturno from *Variants* still haunted the composer's imagination, and again different percussion instruments are set against an almost immobile background. The melodic element is kept to a minimum, with repetition and close intervallic movement, until the preparation for the brief climax. Inevitably the music dissolves with the silence from which it emerged. In its unity and subtle simplicity *Night Music* forms an admirable companion piece to *Variants*.

Hoddinott's interest in the decorative aspects of musical textures was the starting point for *Fioriture*, written in 1968, for full orchestra, again with a formidable array of percussion. He explains the significance of the title in the score:

'The dictionary meaning of "fioriture" is, literally, "flowering": musically, ornamental figures, often extemporized, decorating a melodic outline. It is a term often found in the context of opera and particularly 18th century Italian opera.

From the above it will be obvious that *Fioriture* is essentially a decorative, and therefore a non-developing work. . . . The nature of much of the work is divertimento-like, melodic, and non-contrapuntal.'

In its overall shape *Fioriture* follows the principle of unified multisectional structure established in *Variants*. It is in twenty continuous sections, grouped in five parts, resulting in a very approximate resemblance to an outline consisting of Allegro—Scherzo—Andante—Andante 2—Finale. It is interesting to see what the composer considers to be a 'decorative' texture. In the slower sections the melodic lines take the form of complex arabesques (v. Ex 12), while the sustained chords are overlaid by aleatoric passages on the tuned percussion. The Presto sections have the customary non-decorative impulse, modified certainly by rhythmic syncopation and counterpoint which tend to efface the beat. But they too are embellished by the percussion instruments, and there are some remarkable ensembles involving strings and percussion (Ex 30). The decorative techniques of the 18th

Ex. 30

31

century aria are adapted in the second adagio section; the first violins engage in a simultaneous 'improvised' ornamentation of the second violins' line. Decorative too is the frequent use of 'effects' such as fluttertonguing, tremolo writing, and muted brass and strings. But the work is tautly structured in other respects. The nucleus of both melody and harmony is stated in the opening bar, and all the later material is derived from it. Hoddinott's interest in decoration does not lead him to abandon his fundamental technical procedures, here or elsewhere.

Decorative elements also play a central part in the orchestral composition *The sun, the great luminary of the universe*. This work was commissioned by the Swansea Festival in memory of its founder, Leonard Pinn, in 1970, and its title is taken from a paragraph in James Joyce's *A Portrait of the Artist as a Young Man*:

'The last day had come. The doomsday was at hand. The stars of heaven were falling upon the earth like the figs cast by the fig tree which the wind has shaken. The sun, the great luminary of the universe, had become as sackcloth of hair. The moon was bloodred. The firmament was as a scroll rolled away. The archangel Michael, the prince of the heavenly host, appeared glorious and terrible against the sky. With one foot in the sea and one foot on the land he blew from the archangelical trumpet the brazen death of time. The three blasts of the angel filled all the universe. Time is, time was, but time shall be no more'.

Hoddinott was not of course the first composer to be inspired by the tremendous apocalyptic vision of the end of time. Like Messiaen, he is fully aware of the theological implications, and he quotes the opening line of Bach's chorale 'Es ist genug' towards the end of the work. This chorale and the 'Dies Irae', which is heard in shadowy outline, are the source of the thematic material. But he is also fascinated by the vision itself. Hoddinott is by preference a nocturnal worker, which may well account for his recurrent interest in the sights and sounds of night, and the most dramatic advent of eternal night as portrayed by Joyce has inspired a work which at once relates to the earlier 'night-music' pieces and also surpasses them in colour and intensity. Each section of the work stems from one sentence of the text. A blaze of opening sound, dominated by high brass and resonant percussion, is followed by a quietly desolate passage in which the stars fall, one by one, at random. This extreme contrast sets the bounds of a wide spectrum of colour which is fully explored in the scene that follows. The subject gives rise to some orchestral effects which enlarge the composer's already extensive palette. For example, alternate string and wind chords supply a background to a dialogue between trumpets and percussion, with an elaborately ornamented part on chromatic timpani (Ex 31). Another striking example of Hoddinott's three dimensional writing is quiet alternating chordal background on wind, against which strings, supported by percussion, place full, deep, diatonic chords (Ex 32). The final cadence, now uniting the full orchestra, has the same quiet depth, and, typically, provides less than a full resolution. Hoddinott has pointed out that in *The sun* the music is not conventionally descriptive, but the work leaves no doubt that his personal response to a vividly experienced external stimulus can be a very positive inspiration.

Among the composer's smaller scale orchestral works are the two concerti grossi, a divertimento, and several dance suites. The concerti grossi are intentionally light-weight works. No. 1, in the traditional three movements, is scored for strings with 2 oboes, 2 bassoons and 2 horns, and the solo-tutti concept of the concerto is translated into dialogue between strings and wind, a style underlined by the suggested layout of the orchestra, with strings on one side and wind on the other. The Second Concerto Grosso, written for the National Youth Orchestra of Wales, is more fully scored, but proclaims its essentially divertimento nature in its sequence of six short movements, including an Intrada, an Intermezzo, and an Aria, charmingly scored for 2 flutes, harp and solo violin. The Divertimento op. 69, the most recent composition in this vein, is also designed for reduced wind and strings. Its movements are entitled: amabile, calmo, capriccioso; and its mood is light and graceful to match. The dance suites include two sets of *Welsh Dances* (op. 15 and op. 64), and the *Investiture Dances*, composed to celebrate the Investiture of the Prince of Wales in 1969. For obvious reasons these works are among the composer's best-known and most popular compositions. The note on the score of op. 64 applies to all of them: 'These dances are entirely straightforward entertainment music. There are no actual quotations of folk-tunes; rather the melodies and rhythms are derived from the essential patterns of Welsh folk-music'. Ranging from simple ballad-type melodies to whirling jigs, they are tuneful, imaginative, immediately attractive, and never a note too long. That they are the work of the composer of the symphonies, *Variants* and *The sun* argues not only an extremely versatile technique, but also an almost paradoxically wide-ranging sensibility.

Ex. 31

Ex.ᵗ 32

III THE CONCERTOS

The medium of the concerto has proved as attractive to Hoddinott as that of the symphony, and his compositions in this category include examples for a wide variety of instruments. For a composer so keenly and consistently aware of instrumental colour the concerto offers even more possibilities than the symphony of musical differentiation on a large scale. Hoddinott's concertos and allied works for solo instruments and orchestra embrace most aspects of his musical thought, and are, by and large, strongly individualized, with their character deriving from the composer's conception of the solo instrument.

After the early concertos for clarinet and oboe, both with string orchestra, his first full length work was the Harp Concerto of 1957. The movements are entitled Dialogue, Improvisation, Fantasy. The composer's predilection for the harp is a personal as well as a national one, and, like the other harp works, the concerto reveals his awareness of the limitations which are at once the unique strengths of the instrument. He appreciates the insistent gentleness which makes it the modern successor to Orpheus' lute, and it is this quality which sets the dominant mood from the opening bars of Dialogue. The hesitant rocking phrases of the harp give rise to a chain of melodic ideas in the orchestra, most of them accepting the soloist's preference for ascending stepwise movement (Ex 33). The central climax is reached by a close canonic treatment of one of the harp's initial motifs, and the climax itself is marked by a three-note call on trumpets and drums, also derived from the harp's first phrase. But the soloist takes no part in these dramatic events, and

Ex. 33

re-enters to tame the fury of the orchestra, and lead it back to the tranquillity of the opening. This is one of the most imaginatively handled examples of Hoddinott's palindromic writing. Throughout the movement the textures are clear, and the melodic ideas both distinctive and coherent.

Improvisation is an art to which the harp is particularly suited, and it has traditionally been a touchstone of the performer's skill. But, like impromptu speeches, the best improvisations are the most carefully prepared. In the central movement the harp creates the illusion of improvisation with colouristic effects such as glissandi and broken chords. Again its influence extends to the orchestra, whose related sounds, especially those of the percussion, contribute to the texture. These discontinuous effects alternate and combine with sustained melodic lines, often in the lower registers of the wind instruments, and chords and held notes on brass and strings. The result is a typical Hoddinott combination of surface colour and underlying menace, and gives a new dimension to the expressive potential of the harp.

The Fantasy follows up earlier issues. The first movement is based on D, the second on A flat/G sharp, and this tonal tension is present at the outset in the melodic material. The rhythmic oscillation and stepwise progress of the first movement are resumed, and treated with greater waywardness and impulse. The relationship between soloist and orchestra is explored more extensively than before, the harp establishing its commanding position in solo and antiphonal passages, and in close canonic dialogue with individual members of the orchestra. As in the first movement the soloist remains silent during the build-up to the climax, but joins in with a brilliant flourish to lead to the final resolution on the tonic D.

After the Harp Concerto Hoddinott turned to the keyboard. The first of the three piano concertos, op. 19, was completed early in 1960, some six months after the First Piano Sonata, with which it has some affinities. In four movements, it is scored for piano, wind and percussion. The renunciation of the strings suggests an emphasis on the more forthright, less flexible character associated with the wind band, while the fullness of the percussion department, which includes such esoteric resources as temple blocks, tom-toms, and gong, as well as the more usual components, implies a preoccupation with the corresponding percussive potential of the solo instrument. And in fact the vein of rhetorical lyricism associated with the late 19th and early 20th century piano concerto remains unexploited; the predominant character of the work derives from the orchestral forces selected as well as from the chief protagonist. Nevertheless, although the pianist indeed contributes many strongly percussive passages, the absence of strings allows the soloist to expound melodic phrases in direct contrast to the orchestra, and dialogue of this kind is an important element in the score. Hoddinott postulates his antithesis from the start. In the first movement, Moderato, after a strident opening fanfare from the orchestra, the soloist launches into a virtuosic octave flourish, culminating in a massive interrupted cadence. These follows, quite unexpectedly, a gently flowing piano theme (Ex 34). These two ideas, with a third propounded by the woodwind in their lower register, provide the material for the movement. The second movement, Presto, takes up and develops a textural effect adumbrated in the First Sonata, one which became a hall-mark of Hoddinott's piano idiom. The soloist plays a fast, twisting semiquaver line in the lowest register of the instrument,

Ex.34

doubled at the octave. The wind, also in their lower register, superimpose their own chromatic line in quavers, its irregular phrases punctuated by the percussion. The spare, sombre texture is impetuous and threatening (Ex 35). It builds to a central climax on the orchestra, with the hammered rhythms reinforced by high trills, before returning to its point of departure. Trills characterize the Lento also, as piano and wind embellish each other's soft utterances in a nocturnal evocation. Some aspects of the movement recall the corresponding Adagio of the First Sonata, and both, incidentally, share the same opening and closing chord. But in the Concerto the orchestra resources allow the composer to expand not only the textures but also the thematic treatment. The final Allegro begins by focussing attention on wind and percussion; but the movement is dominated by the tumultuous energy of the solo part.

The Second Piano Concerto followed closely upon the First, and was completed later in the same year. This time Hoddinott wrote for a conventional orchestra, including strings. The work is in three movements. In contrast to no. 1, the opening Moderato begins unobtrusively, almost casually (Ex 36). A number of thematic ideas are presented in dialogue form; individual as they are, they are linked by a common tendency to syncopated rhythm. As the movement moves towards a climax, so the scope of the piano writing is enlarged. The second part of the movement is a varied restatement, ending with a coda by the soloist. Restrained in its overall mood, the movement is marked by an inventive subtlety in the interrelationships of soloist and orchestra, in a wide range of textural combinations.

Ex.35.

Ex. 36

The central Adagio begins as a typical 'night-music' piece, with quiet sustained string chords incorporating the characteristic 'Scotch snap' rhythm (which also opened the Lento of the First Concerto), and coloured by flute and vibraphone. But the atmosphere of stillness is dissipated as the music acquires a new intensity, and the sustained chords of the opening, now asserted forcefully on the brass, become threatening. The piano, in dialogue with the orchestra, persists with a calmer, more detached mood, eventually restoring the opening atmosphere. The concluding Allegro molto again includes a continuous semi-quaver line in the lower compass of the piano, providing a linking thread through thematic interjections by strings and wind. (In a later revision Hoddinott added new counterpoints in this section, modifying the austerity of the original texture).

In several respects the Second Piano Concerto derives from both the Harp Concerto and the First Piano Concerto, with a wider conception of the solo instrument and its potential, embracing its more insinuating as well as its more dramatic qualities.

The Third Piano Concerto dates from 1966, and has affinities with other works of the period in its scoring, which includes a large percussion section, and in the character of its four movements, entitled Cadenza, Scherzo, Notturno, Finale alla Marcia. Four opening chords start the soloist off into a *ff* rhetorical outburst, and thereafter the movement displays the piano in dazzling virtuoso dialogue with the orchestra. The other three movements accord with the composer's general interpretation of their titles. The Scherzo is based on the now familiar bass line and toccata-like figuration in the piano's upper register. The percussion play a vital part in the last two movements, lending individual colour to the textures of the Notturno, and adding to the extroverted display of the march Finale. In its style and exploitation of the solo instrument the Third Concerto was admirably designed for the exceptional gifts of the pianist, John Ogden, who gave the first performance.

Virtuosity is also the hallmark of the Organ Concerto, written in the following year. Hoddinott uses all the power, majesty and brilliance of his solo instrument, and calls for a very large orchestra, including triple wind and a full percussion section, to match the versatility of the organ. The movements constitute another permutation of the composer's favourite types: *I. Toccata 1—Notturno—Toccata 2, II. Variazioni, III. Scherzo alla marcia.* The two protagonists vie with each other in antiphonal dialogue, sometimes over extended phrases and periods, at others alternating chord by chord. The dynamic colour and mood contrasts are extreme, in what is one of the composer's most spectacular scores.

Of the three concerto-like works for solo string instruments, the Violin Concerto is the most straightforward. Written in 1961, immediately after the first two Piano Concertos, it is in four movements: Lento, Allegretto, Adagio, Allegro molto. The two slow movements give the composer the opportunity to contrast different aspects of the violin's lyricism. The dark sonority of the lower compass predominates in the first, which culminates in a richly elaborated cadenza (Ex 37); the clarity of the upper register establishes the character of the second. The Allegretto is a slightly sardonic waltz, while the Allegro molto allows the soloist scope for technical display.

Ex. 37

The Concertino for viola and small orchestra of 1958, despite its nomenclature, is of substantial dimensions, lasting as long in performance as some of the full concertos. The restriction of the orchestral forces to two flutes, two clarinets, two horns and strings, is probably due to a realistic assessment of the viola's limitations in terms of sheer volume and penetration of sound. But Hoddinott does not underestimate the instrument's range of expression. In the opening Andante the viola demonstrates its capacity for sustained *cantabile* playing in all registers, while in the Allegro molto it behaves with uncharacteristic virtuosity, exhibiting its agility in passages of exacting figuration. The last movement is composed of various sections in different tempi and is full of contrasts and dramatic effects. The Concertino constitutes a useful addition to the somewhat exiguous solo repertoire of a still underrated instrument.

In its scale and scope the Nocturnes and Cadenzas for cello and orchestra of 1969 belongs to the concerto category. It is another variation on a familiar theme—the relationship of static and dramatic musical structures. The work is symmetrical in layout, with a Lento and an unaccompanied cadenza preceding a central scherzo, which is followed by another cadenza, and then a concluding Adagio. The arch form is underlined by the ABA disposition of the scherzo, and by a final return of the opening motif, now reordered. The opening motif is also the keystone of the arch, recurring at the central point, the trio of the scherzo. But the musical thought is also progressive. The second cadenza is more urgent and dramatic than the first. The opening Lento is impressionistic, colourful; while the Adagio is quietly meditative, with a continuous lyrical line on the cello, suggesting resolution through serene acceptance.

Another notable contribution to the genre is the Horn Concerto of 1969. Hoddinott had already demonstrated his appreciation of the instrument's versatility in the *Aubade and Scherzo* for horn and strings of 1965. Both the lyrical and joyous aspects of its personality are further explored in the concerto. The title of the first movement, Romanza, is evocative in itself, and the rise and fall of the opening phrase, announced by the soloist without accompaniment, creates a distinctive atmosphere (Ex 38). The orchestra adopts the mood of the soloist, whose lead becomes progressively more affirmative towards the central climax. In the second half the horn continues to dominate with an essentially lyrical line, and brings about the return to the tranquil atmosphere of the opening. Throughout the movement the colour of the solo instrument is enhanced by matching counterpoints on wind and strings, and by the finely calculated use of percussion that characterizes the later style. The result is a varied accompanimental texture, unified by the development of the solo line. In the Scherzo the horn demonstrates its virtuosity in a typical triple time Presto; the tireless soloist sweeps the orchestra through a swiftly moving dance to a crashing halt. Then follows an extended cadenza, in which the soloist meditates upon the earlier material of the work in a section calling for the utmost control and perception on the part of the performer. The opening motif is taken up and resolves into a quiet, sombre cadence on the orchestra.

Ex. 38

IV CHAMBER AND SOLO INSTRUMENTAL MUSIC

Hoddinott's interest in chamber composition dates from his student years, with the String Trio op. 1. This was followed by a Clarinet Quartet in 1953. But his first characteristic work for chamber composition is the Septet, for clarinet, bassoon, horn, violin, viola, cello and pianoforte, of 1956. The Septet was revised in 1973, and this version is now available on record. It is cast in the three movement form typical of the composer at that period, with a central Adagio coming after a Moderato and before an Allegro assai. The general technique relates to that of the other early compositions. The forms are palindromic, the harmonic idiom is still basically tonal, with much chromatic freedom. The melodic shape of the themes and their rhythmic features suggest an influence from Stravinsky's middle period chamber music. It is instructive to observe the nature of the composer's alterations in the later version; these are principally alterations in the scoring. The particular instrumental combination which Hoddinott chose contains three approximately equal and self-contained forces: the wind trio, the string trio, and the pianoforte. In the original version there is frequent doubling between the groups; moreover the scoring is full, with each group contributing its own distinctive idea to a rich texture. These tendencies, combined with a concentration in the middle rather than the extreme compasses of the instruments, lead to a sometimes excessively thick and undifferentiated sound. The revision demonstrates Hoddinott's increasing sensitivity in matters of texture and colour. Doublings are reduced, textures are simplified, and octave transpositions are applied to specific melodic lines. The result is that individual instrumental colours are much more strongly disengaged and the thematic ideas are more clearly distinguishable. This is particularly evident in the Adagio, whose opening bars, formerly scored for the full ensemble, now present a lightly supported duet between clarinet and viola. Without in any way changing the essence of the composition Hoddinott has in this way brought it on to a level with his later works.

Mixed chamber combinations have always been associated with a lighter style, and Hoddinott's next chamber compositions follow this trend. The Sextet for flute, clarinet, bassoon and string trio of 1960, the Variations for flute, clarinet, harp and string quartet of 1962, and the Divertimento for oboe, clarinet, bassoon and horn (1963), are all 'entertainment' music in the 18th century sense. In all of them Hoddinott reflects 18th century practice by showing a preference for shorter movement or sections. The Sextet is in five movements, including a *sotto voce* Moderato, a $\frac{5}{8}$ Scherzo, and a Finale which is itself in five sections of different tempi, but related material, including a march-like Allegro. The Variations are a development of this tendency. They contain eight sections, including a March, Nocturne, a $\frac{5}{8}$ Scherzo, a Waltz, an Elegy and a Pastorale. Hoddinott's choice of instruments inevitably recalls Ravel, and despite obvious differences his Variations have the same sensitivity to instrumental colour and immediacy of appeal. Equally attractive at first hearing is the Divertimento. Its layout of movements: Overture—Scherzo 1—

44

Variations—Scherzo 2—March, recalls the arch-form, especially as the concluding March takes up the main theme of the Overture.

In this little composition Hoddinott is working on a reduced scale. For that very reason perhaps, no other score offers a simpler or more direct approach to many of the essential features of his style. The first theme of the Maestoso, with its anacrusis, the dramatic outline of its initial motif and the subsequent dotted rhythm, contains the seed of many more grandiose openings. The two Scherzi, which are thematically related, are typically fleeting, and quirky—Scherzo 2 is marked prestissimo e sempre *pp*. The central Andante is a continuous set of eight variations on an eight-bar theme, whose derivations from the original are both diverse and easily recognizable; especially attractive are the third variation, a horn solo over trilled accompaniment, and the seventh, a restatement of the theme with interspersed comments by each instrument in turn.

The later Divertimenti for eight instruments (1968) belongs to the same tradition and the titles of its movements again point to both its nature and its provenance: Scherzo I—Canzonetta—Scherzo 2—Barcariola—Scherzo 3. It is in this category of works that we see most clearly the meridional side of the composer's personality—his understanding of simple forms, lyrical melody, bright colours, lively dancing rhythms.

Pages of musical history separate the string quartet from the quartet for wind, and Hoddinott's String Quartet no. 1 (its successor is still to come) is a very different work from the Divertimenti. There are no evocative associations in its section headings. It is played without a break and has the following tempo directions: Grave (tempo 1°)—Allegro molto (tempo 2^{ndo})—Meno Mosso (tempo 3°)—Grave (tempo 1°)—Piu mosso (tempo 3°)—Allegro molto (Tempo 3°). The second half is a development and summation of the earlier material, and the work combines dramatic power and density of working-out. The opening *ff* chords (Ex 39) establish an uncompromising level of dissonance, and the semitone relationship is a notable feature which recurs throughout the work, and informs the melodic as well as the harmonic movement; it is only in the last bar that the dissonances

Ex. 39

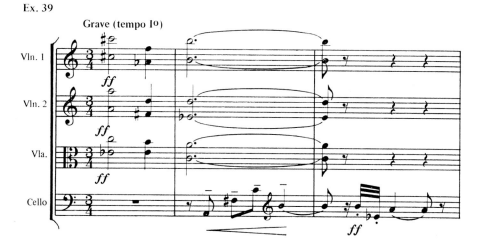

resolve into a unison C sharp. The Grave is a palindrome, with the cello playing the leading rôle in a wide-ranging yet motivically closely-knit rhetorical line. The as yet unresolved C—C sharp relationship at the end of the section provides the starting point for the opening of the Allegro molto, a single line, played *pp*, to whose fleeting movement a nervous intensity is imparted by its irregular division between the four instruments—a characteristically Hoddinottian device (Ex 40). The Meno mosso begins by developing canonic phrases in contrary motion between violin and viola, and the final build-up starts with a close canon between all four instruments (Ex 41). On the whole Hoddinott turns infrequently to classical contrapuntal techniques, and their application here is an indication of his attitude to the medium in what is one of his most demanding works.

Ex. 40

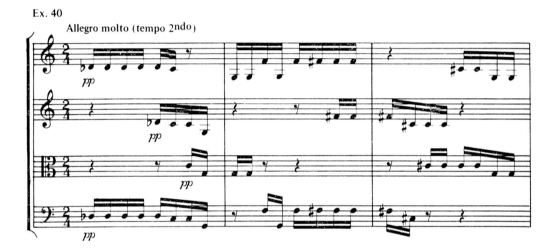

Ex. 41

Although Hoddinott had written four piano sonatas by 1966, he did not turn to the sonata for two instruments until the following year, when he produced the Sonata for clarinet and piano. The work is in three movements: Cadenza, Aria, Moto perpetuo. It shows a freshness of approach to the duo medium, and in particular an emphasis on the individuality of each participant. The clarinet writing is much more demanding than that of Hoddinott's earlier works for the instrument, as the fiercely angular line that opens the sonata may illustrate (Ex 42). The piano does not attempt to emulate this idea; but a later more legato theme is shared between the instruments in a close but rhythmically free canon (Ex 43). This second theme provides the basis for the following Aria, and gives

Ex. 42

Ex. 43

birth to the semitonal movement which predominates in the concluding Moto perpetuo. Contrast of movement types and interrelation of material; aggressively individual shaping of some themes, close integration in others; these are characteristics which recur in the duo sonatas. In 1968 Hoddinott returned to the clarinet again, to deal further with the possibilities of solo expression within a concerted context, in the Nocturnes and Cadenzas for clarinet, violin and cello. The work is continuous; its framework is: Cadenza (cello)—Nocturne 1 (Trio)—Cadenza (violin)—Nocturne 2 (Trio)—Cadenza

(Clarinet)—Coda (Trio). The next duo sonata was the Violin Sonata no. 1, and in the preface to the score he explained his attitude to his medium. 'The title sonata is used here merely to denote two instruments playing together and the work has very little to do with the 19th century sonata, at least structurally.' In this work he evinces his growing preference for a unified multi-sectional form. The sonata is in eleven short sections, all derived from common material which, as the composer remarks, is 'never stated explicitly'. The sections include familiar types, such as Scherzo, Marcia, Cadenza and Romanza, and the recurrent appearance of two ritornelli, varied each time, underlines his allegiance to the Italian baroque rather than to German romanticism. In this sonata, Hoddinott, himself a violinist by training, fully exploits the resources of the instrument, especially in the central cadenza, which combines intensity with thematic relevance.

The same demands are made on the performer in the Violin Sonata no. 2, op. 73 no. 1, dating from 1970. The first movement is again a Cadenza, marked Allegro e brillante, in which rhapsodic flights by the violin are linked and supported by a chordal keyboard part. Despite its apparent freedom, the movement is a closely-knit exploration of the thematic material. The following Moto Perpetuo is also tightly controlled in its structure. The note set, announced simultaneously in natural and inversion forms by the two partners, is used throughout the movement, becoming at one stage an ostinato accompaniment repeated more than twenty times without variation in a procedure unusual in the composer (Ex 44).

Ex. 44

The last movement, Episodi e coda, is another instance of the composer's fondness for summary, condensation and retrospective allusion in his epilogues; the quiet concluding reminiscences of the opening movement invoke a note of nostalgia.

The Cello Sonata of the same year shares an opus number with the Second Violin Sonata. The works are not directly related, but rather complementary. They are linked by the inclusion of a cadenza—in the cello work this section is unaccompanied and forms the second part of the first movement. But Hoddinott's response to the cello's capacities is not primarily to stress its virtuoso capabilities, but rather to underline and to exploit its rich lyrical potential, particularly in its middle register (there is relatively little use made of its upper compass, which is perhaps a refreshing change). The work is in two movements, Andante and Allegro. The texture is clear, and very largely contrapuntal, and thus it lends itself particularly well to closer consideration, as an example of Hoddinott's recent chamber music style. The sonata is based on the following note set (Ex 45). As usual, the row is

Ex. 45

treated as a source of motivic material, rather than an integral 12-note sequence. So, for example, while the piano states the set, omitting one note, at the opening, the cello line develops its expressive melodic curve with a free and selective use of the material in the set. (Ex 46a). A later varied restatement of the opening includes this cello line (Ex 46b); its

Ex. 46

relationship to the original statement is clearly apparent, and at the same time it is a development, in an entirely classical manner, of its prototype. The derivation of this line in the second movement, if not so immediately obvious, is equally certain (Ex 47). Hoddinott has become increasingly concerned to make the perceptibility of his thematic derivations a vital factor in his work.

Ex. 47

Two other features relate the twin op. 73 sonatas: the use of extensive ostinato accompaniment, in this case as a soft chordal background (Ex 48), and a concluding allusion to the opening, summing up in a few bars the whole work.

Ex. 48

By the early seventies it was becoming apparent that the expressive and technical problems posed initially by one set of circumstances could not be fully explored in the context of a single composition, and that Hoddinott was coming more and more to regard his work as a continuous process, with important connections and cross references occurring between different compositions. A logical conclusion was reached when he wrote a set of works on the same material. Four quite different works share the designation op. 78: no. 1, the Third Violin Sonata; no. 2, the Horn Sonata; no. 3, the Sixth Piano Sonata; no. 4, the Piano Quintet. But each of these works has its own individual character. The Third Violin Sonata has some affinity with the earlier Cello Sonata in its opening Moderato, a quietly lyrical movement with a cool two-part contrapuntal texture, in palindromic form. The lines are motivically closely woven, yet fluid in their rhythms and contours. A comparison of the first and second phrases of the violin's opening statement reveals how Hoddinott uses internal motivic variation and repetition to intensify the expression and reach points of climax (Ex 49). The second movement is a *moto perpetuo* Presto, with the violin taking the leading part. The final movement, as in other later works, combines the functions of development and recapitulation. The form, Adagio—Presto, echoes the relationship of the first two movements. In the Adagio the violin engages in a rhapsodic meditation an earlier material: and in the succinct Presto the piano joins the violin on equal terms in another *moto perpetuo* on the basic material.

Ex. 49

The Horn Sonata, like the other two sonatas in the group, is based on G as a tonic. Its family resemblance to the Violin Sonata is evident in the opening movement, Moderato, quasi Allegretto. Like the string sonata, it opens with a long flowing melody which expounds the thematic material for the work and establishes the movement's lyrical character (Ex 50). The qualification in the tempo heading gives rise to contrasting staccato passages, still thematically derived from the opening. The Adagio is improvisatory in style, with arabesques shared between horn and piano.

Ex. 50

The subtlety with which Hoddinott handles his harmony in order to focus attention upon his home tonic may be noticed at the beginning of the final triple time Presto. A twenty-four bar theme is announced by the horn, and is punctuated by the piano at irregular

51

intervals, and apparently at random, with two chords constituting a typical progression (Ex 51). In fact the chords occur only when a note G is sounding in the horn part. So they bring out the tonic note in an otherwise undifferentiated linear pattern, an effect enhanced by their own structure, as appoggiatura chords to a G triad. The rest of the movement provides an exacting test of the performer's intonation, articulation, and breath control. Lyricism, fantasy, agility; all are represented in a work which shows a real understanding of the nature of the instrument.

Ex. 51

The piano quintet, one of the most sonorous combinations in chamber music, has traditionally been the medium for rhetorical, almost orchestral, utterances. There are powerful statements and vivid contrasts in Hoddinott's Piano Quintet. But he does not attempt effects and sonorities beyond the comfortable capabilities of the instruments. When the strings and piano are playing simultaneously, the two forces are distinctively characterized. So, for example, oscillating string chords provide the background to a melodic tone doubled in octaves on the piano; a piano ostinato supports a unison string melody; sustained string chords are embroidered by filigree work on the keyboard. At other times the groups alternate, either in sharing a thematic development, or in establishing various types of dialogue. Formally the quintet depends on the contrast between alternating slow and fast sections. Thematically it is exceptionally direct, with clearly recognizable derivations and restatements. The same qualities characterize the Piano Trio op. 77.

The six piano sonatas constitute the most important group of solo works. There was a time when the piano sonata was the almost exclusive preserve of composers who were themselves accomplished pianists, approaching their task with an innate appreciation of the resources of their medium. In the twentieth century there have been some notable instances of less pianistically endowed composers approaching the problems of writing for solo keyboard as it were from outside and achieving interesting and successful results, partly because they have to adapt a non-pianistic way of thinking. Hoddinott's First Sonata, dating from 1959, bears traces of an essentially orchestral approach. The contrasts of material are often heightened by a change of register. There is an emphasis on the tenor and alto range for the location of expressive melody and there are passages, such as the opening of the Adagio, where a colour contrast between sustained inner parts and adjacent moving lines greater than that available on the keyboard seems to be implied. There is also a reliance on octave passage work, expecially in the bass register, which makes for a mono-linear texture. But there are also other passages which show a keen awareness of specifically pianistic sonorities, and the musical ideas in all four movements are crisp and succinct.

The Second Sonata marks an advance on the first. The centrepiece is the Adagio, a concentrated exploration of the expressive content of certain melodic intervals in different contexts. It is framed by a Moderato, based on a juggling of short melodic and rhythmic motives, and an Allegro, in Hoddinott's slightly ironical march style. The Third Sonata of 1965 reflects the composer's desire to move away from more conventional formal divisions. It depends on two tempi, in obvious contrast, presented alternately, with direct thematic links between their respective material. The latter stages of the movement create the effect of a summing up and integration of the earlier contrasts. The piano-writing is increasingly individual, with further exploitation of the bass register, and this use of timbre is, as John Ogdon has pointed out in an introductory note to the score, clearly related to the piano writing of the Third Piano Concerto.

The Fourth and Fifth Sonatas date from 1966 and 1968, and they underline Hoddinott's interest in Baroque forms. No. 4 comprises three Toccatas, separated by an Aria and a Notturno; and no. 5 consists of two Arias, preceded by a Cadenza and followed by a Toccata. The rhapsodic nature of the Toccata allows the maximum use of keyboard effects, as well as dramatic contrasts of material, compass, and texture, and Hoddinott's writing here is both rich and exacting. The texture of the Arias, despite the implications of the title, is far from simple. There is indeed at the heart of them a strong lyrical impulse, and an accompanimental element; but Hoddinott is equally concerned with the improvised ornamental aspect of the traditional aria, and he applies ornamentation to both melodic and chordal elements in luxuriant profusion, with broken chords, trills, glissandi, in all registers of the keyboard. A comparison between these movements and the slow sections of the first sonatas will show at once how far he has developed a colouristic conception of keyboard writing.

The most recent sonata, no. 6, belongs to the op. 78 group of works. Dedicated to the memory of Alan Rawsthorne, it is remarkable for its concise intensity, and for features of almost programmatic character. It is in one continuous movement, lasting ten minutes. The first section, Adagio maestoso, recalls Debussy both in spirit and method, despite

obvious differences of idiom. It is based on four motifs. The opening bars consist of
tolling bass chords, answered by a clangorous progression in the treble (Ex 52). This is
followed by a gentle melodic phrase, also antiphonally divided (Ex 53). Two other motifs
are introduced, a chord progression in irregular rhythm (Ex 54) and a supple melodic line,
reminiscent of Debussy's Delphic dancers (Ex 55). The section is composed of a succession

of phrases, inaugurated by a variant of one or other of these motifs, which brings them together in new relationships, whose momentum tends to dissolve into trills and arabesques. Out of this deliquescence the Allegro bruscamente establishes hard rhythmic outlines and, despite a variety of textures including passages in major ninths (Ex 56) and counterpoints in clashing octaves, drives forward to a *sffz* return of the opening bass D. The first treble chord is sustained, and resolves into a quietly stated chorale, twelve bars long (Ex 57). Eight further bars, during which the opening motifs re-emerge and resolve into the final D, provide a reflective coda to a most impressive composition.

Ex. 56

Ex. 57

Hoddinott's other solo works include a Sonata, a Suite, and a Fantasy for harp, a Toccata alla giga and an Intrada for organ, and a Sonatina for clavichord.

V THEATRE, CHORAL AND SOLO VOCAL MUSIC

One of the most far-reaching influences on Welsh musical life in recent years has been the creation and establishment of a National Opera company. It is a part of the company's policy to promote the work of contemporary Welsh composers, and Hoddinott's opera, *The Beach of Falesá*, was commissioned by the Welsh National Opera, and given its first performance on 26 March, 1974, at the New Theatre, Cardiff, thereby becoming the first full-length opera by a Welsh composer to be mounted by the National company. It was not Hoddinott's first contact with the theatre. Earlier works include a masque, *The Race of Adam*, and incidental music for stage and broadcast drama. But the Welsh National Opera commission allowed him the opportunity to fulfil a long cherished amibition to produce a full-scale work for the opera house.

The libretto by Glyn Jones is founded on a short story by R. L. Stevenson, and is in three acts. The opera is set in Falesá, an island of the South Pacific. In Act 1 Wiltshire, a new trader, arrives by schooner. He is welcomed by the resident trader, Case, who persuades him, in his own interests, to go through a fake wedding ceremony with a native girl Uma, selected by Case, that same afternoon. The ceremony takes place amid celebrations, and Wiltshire, who has fallen in love with his bride at first sight, determines to regard the marriage as a real one. Act 2 begins a month later. None of the natives will trade with the now despondent Wiltshire. Uma confides to the Catholic priest, Father Galuchet, that she may be the cause of the boycott. Case, she believes, has placed a tabu on her, by falsely pretending that she has broken a promise to marry one of the native chiefs from another island. The priest persuades her to tell Wiltshire of her suspicions, and this she does. Wiltshire goes to Case and accuses him of putting a tabu on Uma. Scornfully, Case rejects the charge, and offers to take the matter up with the Council of Chiefs. In the final scene of the act Case, in conference with the Chiefs, loses his temper with one of them, Maea, and storms out. Wiltshire confronts him and, as they quarrel, accuses Case of responsibility for the deaths of earlier trading rivals. In Act 3, a few days later, Maea comes to Wiltshire's store and offers to trade with him. Wiltshire accepts, and discloses that he has discovered in the woods the 'temple' of evil spirits constructed by Case to maintain his hold upon the natives through superstition. He is determined to destroy it and expose Case. In the final scene Wiltshire approaches the temple by night and wrecks the mechanical devices and grotesque figures he finds there. Uma has followed him, and they are both confronted by Case, who is armed. Case fires at them. The wounded Wiltshire manages to drag Case to the ground and stab him. Dying, Case proclaims his philosophy, that Wiltshire must come to resemble him. Wiltshire and Uma are reunited.

In adapting Stevenson's story the librettist has made some alterations. Lesser characters, such as Case's servant, Black Jack, and Uma's mother, Faavao, are more fully developed in the opera, making for a more varied grouping of personalities. Stevenson's missionary, Tarleton, is omitted and his functions allotted to Father Galuchet. But the most fundamental change is the switch of emphasis from Wiltshire to Case as the central character. Stevenson's Case is ruled solely by greed and consequent jealousy towards any potential rival. The operatic Case is a more equivocal and complicated figure. In his final vehement monologue he reveals that his motivation is love of power itself.

> 'Dominate
> or die—this became my guiding faith.
> Not trade not copra, not greed, impelled me on,
> But *will*, the iron will to stand alone,
> To stand supreme, unequalled, feared,
> Self-sufficient, lord!'

Stevenson's original is, as one would expect from a master story-teller, a splendid traveller's yarn. Its strength lies in its incident and action; it contains neither shading nor development of character. The modification of Case's character in the libretto is an attempt to give an added psychological dimension to the plot: to move from melodrama, the straightforward confrontation of good and evil, with a happy ending, to tragedy, the self-destruction of a flawed hero. But the practical effect of this change is limited by the fact that Case's true nature does not emerge gradually in the course of the opera. As a result the potential tensions of the situation are not realized, and there is little scope for psychological movement in the interaction of the protagonists. If the opera is in this sense static, however, there are passages of convincing emotional portrayal. Hoddinott remarked, in an interview before the first performance, 'This is a romantic story and the music must follow'. And it is in the love music that the characters come most vividly to life: the tender song of Uma in Act 1, recalling her childhood, which captivates Wiltshire (Ex 58), and the

Ex. 58

brief duet between the two lovers in Act 3. And, above all, there is evocation of atmosphere and environment. Hoddinott avoids all obviously South Pacific effects; but his rich orchestral textures and in particular his mastery of percussion colours are very suited to the creation of an exotic ambience. Certain evocations remain in the memory: the opening scene on board the schooner, as the tropical dawn lightens the sky and the song of kanakas is heard, distantly at first, then gradually becoming louder; the closing scene of the same act, with the marriage song of the natives ending the ceremony as daylight fades; the nocturnal sounds, precise yet vaguely menacing, of the forest surrounding the evil shrine of Case.

The musical techniques follow the composer's usual methods. A twelve-note set provides much of the thematic material, and a number of leit-motifs derived from the set play a part in the dramatic characterization. A tonal tension based on the tritone E flat—A embodies the conflict of Wiltshire and Case. The vocal lines are in a free arioso style ranging from recitative to lyrical melody.

André Gide once said that he wrote, not to be read, but to be re-read. A similar point of view might well be expressed by the contemporary composer of opera, faced with the complexities of the genre, and the attendant problems of immediate communication with his audience through a modern idiom. It is to be hoped that there will be an early opportunity to reassess *The Beach of Falesá*. In the meantime Hoddinott has completed other operatic compositions, and it seems likely that this side of his activity will continue to develop in the future.

Hoddinott's most ambitious choral work, *The Tree of Life*, for soprano and tenor soloists, chorus and orchestra, was commissioned by the Three Choirs Festival, and performed in August 1971 at Gloucester Cathedral. The text is by W. Moelwyn Merchant. It is based on the venerable Christian tradition, identifying 'the Tree in the midst of Paradise', which bore the fruit of the Fall of Man, with the redeeming Cross of Christ, and on the associated Golden Legend, linking the Tree of Paradise, the rejected beam of Solomon's temple, the Cross of Christ and the healing Tree of Life, growing in the New Jerusalem, as foreseen in the book of Revelation. The author has skilfully woven together original material with passages from the Scriptures and extracts from English metaphysical poets, into a text which falls into six parts, with a Prologue.

Part 1. The Tree of Life. The story of the Fall.

Part 2. The Tree of Seth. Adam's son plants three seeds from the Tree of Life under his dead father's tongue.

Part 3. Solomon's Temple. The Tree growing on Adam's grave is prepared as the main beam for the new temple of Solomon, and discarded.

Part 4. The Pool of Siloam. The rejected Tree has dammed the river's flow, creating a Pool.

Part 5. The Crucifixion. The carpenter charged with making the Cross of Christ uses the Tree from the Pool of Siloam.

Part 6. The New Jerusalem. The vision of St. John the Divine.

The Prologue establishes the paradox at the heart of the legend.

> 'Adam sinned and died
> Christ sinned not, yet died;
> This is strange and wonderful.
> Paradise and Calvary,
> Christ's Cross and Adam's tree, stood in one place;'

The difficulties inherent in writing a modern oratorio text based on scriptural tradition are immense. The author must reconcile biblical and contemporary modes of expression. He must propound a theme, if not a theology, which is acceptable to present day audiences. He must also, of course, offer the composer opportunity for musical treatment of the text. By all these criteria Merchant's libretto is a very good one. It moves smoothly from one verbal style to another. It develops coherently an essentially simple yet far-reaching theme. It allows for contrasted treatment of the sections, and presents a variety of scenes and images which lend themselves admirably to musical translation.

Hoddinott responds fully to his opportunities. The overall layout of the work has affinities with his symphonic structures. The Prologue with Parts 1 and 2 form a first movement, with a slow introduction. Part 3 is a scherzo, Part 4 a slow movement. Parts 5 and 6, with varying tempi, including a return ot the opening, is a multi-sectional finale. A further parallel to Hoddinott's symphonic writing lies in thematic transference from section to section. The same music used in Part 3 for 'O how amiable' is recalled before the end to the text 'O quam gloriosum' (Ex 59). The opening bars of the Prologue recur

Ex. 59

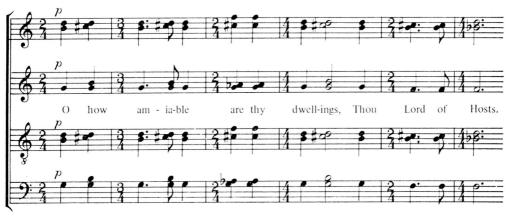

in Part 3, and provide the main material for Part 4. The motives undergo the same processes of variation and extension as those of the instrumental compositions; the main scherzo theme of Part 3 is particularly susceptible to alteration (Ex 60).

The chorus have the customary multiple rôle to play in the work. They act as narrator, protagonists, and commentators. The choral idiom is consequently widely varied. Sometimes the chorus sing a chromatic line in unison, accompanied or unaccompanied. More frequently they move in two contrapuntal lines, doubled at the octave (Ex 61). The chordal writing is mostly of two kinds: mono-triadic, with dissonance added by auxiliary notes (v. Ex 59); bi-triadic, with two triadic lines moving in contrary motion (Ex 62). In either case each individual line is relatively easy for the choral performer to negotiate. Hoddinott is also aware of the effectiveness of simple, open chords in an otherwise dissonant context (Ex. 63).

The writing for solo voices is exacting, and ranges from recitative through largely syllabic melodic curves to florid melismata of descriptive and dramatic significance. When the text demands, the flexible idiom can flower into lyricism, whose restrained intensity conveys awe as well as emotion (Ex 64).

Ex. 60

Ex. 61

Throughout the oratorio the orchestra enhances the moods. The full orchestra embodies the barbaric splendour of Solomon's temple; the solemn notes of the trombones accompany the great voice proclaiming 'I am Alpha and Omega, the first and the last'; the sinuous wind depicts the serpent in the garden; and, most movingly of all, high strings and flute evoke the gentle stillness of Siloam's waters.

Ex. 62

Pa - ra -dise and   Cal - va - ry; Christ's   Cross and A- dam's tree

stood   in   one   place.

Ex. 63

Out of this de - sert   pass to Pa - ra   dise; There at the gate of the

fla -ming sword   Ask the   way to the   Tree.

Ex. 64

(Andante)

The   an - gel   of   God   stood a-side for his   pass-ing

And Seth stood in Pa - ra - dise   Which no man had seen since A -dam's   sin

61

The shorter choral works cover a wide spectrum, and include a number of substantial compositions. *Black Bart*, a ballad for mixed voices and orchestra, is a suitably extroverted setting, employing a wide range of vocal effects, of a poem on the legendary pirate captain, a Welsh counterpart to Drake. *Dives and Lazarus* is a cantata for two soloists, mixed chorus and orchestra on a dramatic text beginning 'Weep and howl, ye rich men'. Several unaccompanied pieces have as their theme legendary or historical scenes of violence. *Danegeld* is based on episodes from the epic, the Battle of Maldon. The ballad *Rebecca* is the defiant song of rioters protesting against toll taxes in 19th century Wales. The *scena*, *An Apple Tree and a Pig* is drawn from Arthurian legend and deals with Merlin's horror after his unwitting murder of his sister's son. The idiom of these works is direct, forceful, generally syllabic, and either chordal or based on a two-part texture, with strong rhythmic contours, and wide ranging dynamics (Ex 65).

Ex. 65

Violence, refined into sophisticated personal cruelty, is again the subject of one of the composer's most unusual scores, the *scena* for solo soprano and instrumental ensemble, *Roman Dream*. The text is by Emyr Humphreys, who also wrote *An Apple Tree and a Pig*. The poem is spoken by an intelligent, well-meaning philosopher from the Roman court who is being hunted to death at the casual whim of a bored emperor. The author describes it as 'a narrative poem . . . cast in the form of a dream—or a nightmare', and conceives the plot as having 'a mythical power . . . sustaining a growth of meaning that should bring it within our contemporary experience'. Hoddinott's setting was written for the Paris Chamber Ensemble, with Josephine Nendick as soloist, and was given its first performance in the French capital, in 1968. So it is hardly surprising that it is related to the style of French post-serialism, exemplified by Boulez' *Le Marteau sans maître*, in its use of the instrumental ensemble, comprising piano and harp as well as a percussion department which includes such exotica as African log drums and a Mexican bean. If the instrumental texture is predominantly pointillist, the vocal line on the other hand is expressionist in its wide curves, its abrupt dynamic switches, its changes of vocal colour, specified in the score. It is precisely that juxtaposition of the impersonal kaleidoscopic texture of the accompaniment and the emotional intensity of the solo line that conjures up the atmosphere of nightmare horror that was the poet's aim, a horror prolonged into silence by the lonely voice and the final instrumental shiver.

At the other extreme are the arrangements of *Four Welsh Songs*, for male voices and orchestra or piano, settings which match the instrumental dances in their adept treatment of modal melodies and harmonies. The church music includes various short anthems, carols, and an unaccompanied motet entitled *Out of the Deep*. The text of the motet is arranged by W. M. Merchant and contains extracts from the psalm De Profundis, and from Donne and Shirley. Some of the musical techniques employed recall the rhythmic and contrapuntal methods of the medieval period (Ex 66).

Ex. 66

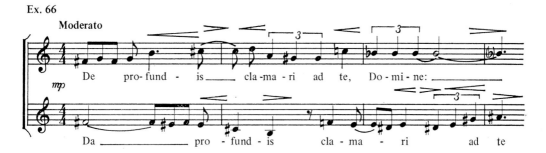

It is only recently that Hoddinott has turned to song composition, with two cycles for voice and piano, *Ancestor Worship*, and *Landscapes*. These songs mark another collaboration with the Anglesey writer Emyr Humphreys. *Ancestor Worship* celebrates the dead: the ordinary people who carved poetry out of their own flesh; the warrior youth destined to be slain in battle; the weary, tender ghost of a father; the leader planning the preservation of his people. *Landscapes* deals with five places in Anglesey: a mountain, a stretch of coastline, and three ruined sites—a fortified village, an island refuge, a headland chapel. Although the cycles are independent, the same complementary themes run through both: present and past; growth and decay; action and reflection; conflict and reconciliation.

When the writer Jules Renard asked Ravel what he thought his musical settings could add to the prose poems of the *Histoires Naturelles*, the composer replied that he did not hope to add anything, but would try to interpret faithfully in music the writer's meaning. Humphrey's poems, like those of Renard, are complex and self-contained. Like Ravel, Hoddinott allows the text to speak for itself, through a flexible vocal line which respects the natural rhythms and inflections of speech. The poems are full of concrete imagery.

Hoddinott does not attempt to match each phase of the text. He distils the essence of the key concepts into a musical idea, whether it be stillness, exultation, or the song of a skylark high above a ruined chapel (Ex 67). The accompaniments develop motivically, assuring background continuity to the vocal line. In three songs versions of Hoddinott's favourite trochaic rhythm suggest timelessness (Ex 68). The ripple on the mirroring water inspires a further variant (Ex 69).

Although the poems of Humphreys are not of the kind that are obviously apt for musical setting, Hoddinott's language is well suited to their density, their harsh lyricism and their unsentimental evocations.

Ex. 67

Ex. 68

(a) Andante

Adagio

(b)

(c) Andante

Ex. 69
  Adagio

POSTSCRIPT

There can be no conclusion to a study of a living composer, especially one as creatively active as Hoddinott. It would be premature to undertake an evaluation of his work in comparative terms, and rash to make predictions about his future development. But one thing may be said with confidence. However we may respond to it, his is a recognizably individual voice.

Some of Hoddinott's music is sunlit. *Fioriture* sparkles with Mediterranean colour. The chamber music for wind ensemble is open, extrovert. The *Welsh* and *Investiture Dances* have a sociable gaiety entirely in keeping with a side of the composer's life and personality familiar to all who know him. But much of his music is, to use his own favourite term, nocturnal. It expresses the solitude of midnight, the insidious obsessions of the long night watches, the desolation of the darkest hour. Night is the time of insomnia, of nameless fears, of sudden violence. Man who has eaten of the Tree of Life can no longer rest in God's quiet night. The Rebecca rioters march when the sun is down, their flaming torches burning holes in the darkness. The defeated Case dies in the flickering glow from his smouldering temple. The Roman philosopher flees in anguish through the night, knowing he will be slain before dawn. In the long winter nights pity and terror seize the soul of the tormented Merlin, and he longs for death.

At night the aural perceptions are heightened. Silence becomes audible and time is additive, each irregular segment defined by isolated events in sound. At night the stars fall, the archangelical trumpet blows the death of time. Time is, time was, but time shall be no more.

In a note on the recording of *The sun, the great luminary of the universe* Hoddinott refers to 'contrasts of explosive impact and massive stillness'. There could be no better definition of the boundaries of his vision. His work is an unremitting exploration of the intervening territory.

APPENDIX I

CATALOGUE OF WORKS

OPERA

Op.	Title	Libretto	Date	Publisher
83	The Beach of Falesá	Glyn Jones, from the story by R. L. Stevenson	1970–74 (1st perf. Cardiff, 1974)	OUP
88	The Magician	John Morgan	1975 (1st perf. ITV 11.2.76)	OUP

ORCHESTRAL MUSIC (without soloist)

Op.	Title	Date	Publisher
4, no. 2	Fugal Overture	1952	OUP
5	Nocturne	1952	OUP
7	Symphony no. 1	1955	OUP
13	Serenade for str	1957	OUP
15	Welsh Dances (Set 1)	1958	OUP
—	Two Welsh Nursery Tunes	1959	OUP
—	Entry	1960	Mills
—	Folksong Suite	1962	OUP
29	Symphony no. 2	1962	OUP
31	Variations	1962	Novello
34	Sinfonia for str	1964	OUP
35	Overture: Jack Straw	1964	OUP
41	Concerto Grosso	1965	OUP
45	Overture: Pantomime	1966	OUP
46	Concerto Grosso no. 2	1966	OUP
47	Variants	1966	OUP
48	Night Music	1966	OUP
56	Sinfonietta	1968	OUP
60	Fioriture	1968	OUP
61	Symphony no. 3	1968	OUP
64	Welsh Dances (Set 2)	1969	OUP
66	Investiture Dances	1969	OUP

Op.	Title	Date	Publisher
67	Sinfonietta 2	1969	OUP
69	Divertimento	1969	OUP
70	Symphony no. 4	1969	OUP
71	Sinfonietta 3	1970	OUP
72, no. 1	Suite no. 1	1970	OUP
76	'The sun, the great luminary of the universe'	1970	OUP
72, no. 3	Sinfonietta 4	1971	OUP
72, no. 4	Aubade	1972	OUP
72, no. 5	'the hawk is set free'	1972	OUP
72, no. 6	'the floore of heaven'	1973	OUP
81	Symphony no. 5	1973	OUP
86	Landscapes / Tirlun	1975	OUP
—	Welsh Airs and Dances for Symphonic wind band	1975	OUP

ORCHESTRAL MUSIC (with soloists)

Op.	Title	Date	Publisher
3	Concerto for cl and str	1950	OUP
8	Concerto for ob and str	1955	OUP
11	Harp Concerto	1957 (rev. 1970)	OUP
14	Concertino for va and small orchestra	1958	OUP
16, no. 2	Nocturne and Dance for harp and orchestra	1959	OUP
19	Concerto for pf, wind and percussion	1960	OUP
21	Piano Concerto no. 2	1960	OUP
22	Violin Concerto	1961	OUP
42	Aubade and Scherzo for hn and orchestra	1965	OUP
44	Piano Concerto no. 3	1966	OUP
51	Organ Concerto	1967	OUP
62	Nocturnes and Cadenzas for vc and orchestra	1969	OUP
65	Horn Concerto	1969	OUP
72, no. 2	Concertino for tpt, hn, and orchestra	1971	OUP
85	Ritornelli for trbn and small orchestra	1974	OUP

CHORAL MUSIC

Op.	Title	Date	Publisher
—	Carol (words by L. C. Huws) for SA and pf	1952	Carolau Hen a Newydd (NFMS)
—	Codiad Lloer (words by G. Jones) for TB	1958	University of Wales Press
—	Great art Thou, O God (Anthem, words by Gwynno James)	1961	OUP
23	The Race of Adam (Masque, words by W. M. Merchant) for STrTB, narrator, chorus, boys' voices, org. and orchestra	1961	MS
25	Carol (words by L. C. Huws) for female voices	1961	OUP
26	Rebecca (words by J. M. White) for unaccompanied chorus	1961	OUP
24	Job (Oratorio, words arr. A. T. Davies) for B, chorus and orchestra	1959–62	OUP
30	Three Medieval Songs (trans. C. Elliott) for SSA unaccompanied	1962	OUP
—	Everyman's work shall be made manifest (Anthem) for SATB and org.	1964	OUP
—	Introit (words by Bishop Heber) for SATB	1964	OUP
33	Danegeld (words by R. G. Thomas) for SATB	1964	OUP
38, no. 1	What tidings? (Carol, words by J. Audeley) for SATB unaccompanied	1964	OUP
39	Dives and Lazarus (Cantata, words by G. James) for SBar, chorus, org, pf duet, and orchestra	1964	OUP
55	An Apple Tree and a Pig (words by E. Humphreys) for SATB unaccompan'ed	1968	OUP
59	Barti Ddu (Black Bart) (words by J. D. Hooson) for chorus and orchestra	1968	OUP
—	Eryri (words by T. H. Parry-Williams) for Bar, chorus and orchestra	1969	OUP
74	Out of the Deep (Motet, words by W. M. Merchant) for SATB unaccompanied	1970	OUP
75	Voyagers (Cantata, words by J. M. White) for bar. solo, male chorus and orchestra	1970–6	OUP
79	The Tree of Life (Oratorio, words by W. M. Merchant) for ST, chorus, org and orchestra	1971	OUP

Op.	Title	Date	Publisher
—	Puer Natus (Carol) for SATB and org	1971	OUP
—	Four Welsh Songs (words trad.) for male choir and orchestra (or pf)	1971	OUP
80	St. Paul on Malta (Cantata, words by Paul Merchant) for T, chorus and orchestra	1971	MS
—	Ieunctid y Dydd (Youth of the Day) (words by Sir T. H. Parry-Williams) for chorus and orchestra	1972	MS
84	The Silver Swimmer (words by J. M. White) for SATB and pf duet	1973	OUP
—	Two Welsh Songs for mixed voices and pf	1975	OUP
—	To Autumn (Keats) for mixed voices	1976	OUP

KEYBOARD MUSIC

Op.	Title	Date	Publisher
9	Nocturne no. 1 for pf	1956	MS
16, no. 1	Nocturne no. 2 for pf	1959	Novello
17	Piano Sonata no. 1	1959	OUP
18	Sonatina for clavichord (or pf)	1959	Stainer & Bell
27	Piano Sonata no. 2	1962	Novello
37, no. 1	Toccata alla giga for org	1964	OUP
40	Piano Sonata no. 3	1965	Novello
37, no. 2	Intrada for org	1966	OUP
49	Piano Sonata no. 4	1966	OUP
57	Piano Sonata no. 5	1968	OUP
37 no. 3	Sarum Fanfare for org	1970	OUP
78 no. 3	Piano Sonata no. 6	1972	OUP

INSTRUMENTAL AND CHAMBER MUSIC

Op.	Title	Date	Publisher
1	String Trio	1949	MS
6	Clarinet Quartet	1953	MS
10	Septet for cl, bn, hn, v, va, vc, and pf	1956	MS
12, no. 1	Rondo Scherzoso for tpt and pf	1957	OUP
12, no. 2	Rondo Capriccioso for trbn and pf	1957	MS
20	Sextet for fl, cl, bn, v, va and vc	1960	OUP
28	Variations for fl, cl, harp and str quartet	1962	OUP
32	Divertimento for ob, cl, bn, and hn	1963	OUP

Op.	Title	Date	Publisher
36	Sonata for harp	1964	OUP
43	String Quartet no. 1	1965	OUP
—	Arabesque for v and pf	1966	GPWM
50	Sonata for cl and pf	1967	OUP
52	Suite for harp	1967	OUP
53	Nocturnes and Cadenzas for cl, v and vc	1968	OUP
58	Divertimenti for fl, cl, bn, hn, v, va, vc and db	1968	OUP
63	Sonata no. 1 for v and pf	1969	OUP
68, no. 1	Nocturnes and Cadenzas for harp	1969	MS
68, no. 2	Fantasy for harp	1970	OUP
73, no. 1	Sonata no. 2 for v and pf	1970	OUP
73, no. 2	Sonata for vc and pf	1970	OUP
77	Piano Trio	1970	MS
78, no. 1	Sonata no. 3 for v and pf	1971	OUP
78, no. 2	Sonata for hn and pf	1971	OUP
78, no. 4	Quintet for pf and str	1972	OUP
89	Sonata no. 4 for v and pf	1976	OUP

SONGS

2	Two Songs of Fletcher, for bass and pf	1950	MS
4, no. 1	Lullaby (anon), for medium voice and pf	1950	MS
38, no. 2	Medieval Carol medium voice and org/pf	1965	OUP
54	Roman Dream (E. Humphreys) Scena for soprano and instrumental ensemble	1968	OUP
82	Ancestor Worship (E. Humphreys) cycle for high voice and pf	1972	MS
87	Five Landscapes Ynys Mon (E. Humphreys) cycle for tenor and pf	1975	OUP
90	A Contemplation upon Flowers 3 songs for soprano and orchestra 1. Life (G. Herbert) 2. The Flower (G. Herbert) 3. A Contemplation upon Flowers (H. King)	1976	OUP

INCIDENTAL MUSIC

Title	Date
Radio play: There go the ships	1950
,, ,, St. David	1951
,, ,, Dan Owen and the angel Jal	1951
,, ,, Jet-age metal	1952
,, ,, Richard Savage (Gwyn Jones)	1953
,, ,, The Time Barrier	1954
,, ,, The Meeting (Dannie Abse)	1956
Blood Wedding (Lorca)	1957
The Firstborn (Fry)	1958
Radio play: Esther (Saunders Lewis)	1959
Film: Pembrokeshire, my county	1960
,, The Sword of Sherwood Forest	1960
,, The Horse-masters	1961
Jackie the Jumper (Gwyn Thomas)	1962
Antigone (Anouilh)	1963
TV play: Blodeuwedd (Saunders Lewis)	1964
The Pied Piper (Browning)	1966
Film: The Secret World of Odilon Redilon	1973
,, Steel be my Sister	1976

APPENDIX II

GRAMOPHONE RECORDINGS

Title	Performer(s)	Label	Number
Symphony no. 2 Variants	L.S.O. cond. del Mar	Pye Virtuoso	TPLS 13013
Symphony no. 3 'the sun, the great luminary'	L.S.O. cond. Atherton	Decca	SXL 6570
Symphony no. 5 Concerto for horn and orchestra Concerto no. 2 for piano and orchestra	L.S.O. Tuckwell, Jones cond. Davis	Decca	SXL 6606
Concerto for harp and orchestra Concerto for clarinet and strings	L.S.O. Ellis, de Peyer cond. Atheron	Decca	SXL 6513
Welsh Dances—1st Set	R.P.O. cond. Groves	EMI	ASD 2739
Welsh Dances—2nd Set	NYOW cond. Davison	MFP	2129
Welsh Dances—2nd Set Investiture Dances	NYOW cond. Davison	BBC Enterprises	REC 222
Sinfonietta I Night Music Concertino for viola and chamber orchestra Cantata: Dives and Lazarus	N.P.O. Erdelyi, Felicity Palmer Thomas Allen, W.N.O. Chorale cond. Atherton	Argo	ZRG 824
String Quartet Sonata for clarinet and piano	Cardiff University Ensemble, de Peyer, Harrison	Pye	GSGC 14107
Sonata for cello and piano	Isaac, Tryon	Argo	ZRG 695
Sonata for horn and piano	Tuckwell, Peters		CF 3054–2 (U.S.A.)
Roman Dream Piano Trio	Festival Players, Margaret Price, Lockhart	Argo	ZRG 691

BIBLIOGRAPHY

M. Boyd: 'The Beach of Falesá', *Musical Times*, vol. 115, (1974), p. 207

B. Hesford: 'The piano works of Alun Hoddinott', *Musical Opinion*, vol. 89, (1965–6), p. 411

A. Hoddinott: 'Composers' forum', *London Musical Events*, vol. 13 no. 8, (August 1958), p. 25; vol. 22, no. 5, (May 1967), p. 10

N. Kay: 'Hoddinott's variants', *Tempo*, no. 79, (Winter 1966–7), p. 15.

K. Loveland: 'A year of rich promise for a Welsh composer', *Music and Musicians*, vol. 8, no. 6, (February 1960), p. 9

K. Loveland: 'Alun Hoddinott', *South Wales*, (Spring 1970), p. 32

C. Powell: 'Hoddinott's first opera', *Music and Musicians*, vol. 22, no. 7, (March 1974), p. 20

C. Raybould: 'Contemporary Welsh composers', *The Welsh Anvil*, vol. 5, (1953), p. 32

H. F. Redlich: 'Alun Hoddinott', *Die Musik in Geschichte und Gegenwart*, Kassel, Bärenreiter, (1957), Bd. 6, col. 503

C. B. Rees: 'Alun Hoddinott', *London Musical Events*, vol. 13, no. 12, (December 1958), p. 14

A. F. L. Thomas: 'Alun Hoddinott', *Musical Times*, vol. 96, (1955), p. 523

S. Walsh: 'Two new British operas: Stephen Walsh talks to Alun Hoddinott and Gordon Crosse', *Listener*, vol. 91, (14 March 1974), p. 344

D. Wynne: 'Alun Hoddinott', *Anglo-Welsh Review*, vol. 13, (1965), p. 44

D. Wynne: 'Alun Hoddinott: a survey', *Welsh Music*, vol. 3, no. 8, (Winter 1970), p. 2

Younger Generation, *The*: 'Alun Hoddinott', *Musical Times*, vol. 101, (1960), p. 148